A RED TIDE IN WINTER

S. Sweeney Reilly

Bloomington, IN  Milton Keynes, UK

authorHOUSE®

AuthorHouse™
1663 Liberty Drive, Suite 200
Bloomington, IN 47403
www.authorhouse.com
Phone: 1-800-839-8640

AuthorHouse™ UK Ltd.
500 Avebury Boulevard
Central Milton Keynes, MK9 2BE
www.authorhouse.co.uk
Phone: 08001974150

First published by AuthorHouse 11/15/2006

ISBN: 978-1-4259-5852-7 (sc)

Library of Congress Control Number: 2006909676

Printed in the United States of America
Bloomington, Indiana

This book is printed on acid-free paper.

Dedicated to my husband Paul–
whose love and support are never-ending

Authors Note

As an art historian for over twenty years, it's safe to say that art has changed my life. It ranks right up there with the sudden deaths of my mother, father, brother, and my young niece and nephew as a life-altering learning experience. Art imitates life at every turn, but then rewards and presents us with new views of reality. It truly is a beautiful world we live in, even when family tragedies hit harder and harder. I tell my students, in order to understand about life and death, the universal themes, rights and wrongs, look at art. Its powerful images are an unforgettable emotional and awe-inspiring experience. Open your minds, study the details, and knowledge follows. Well, only time will tell, and reveal to us who the listeners were in my classes, but maybe this book will help them and others along the way towards respect and reverence for life and art.

When my twelve-year-old niece lived her last year in a hospital bed, she still traveled the world—through art. Forgetting that she was sick and probably dying, she saw in art all that was beautiful and tragic, like herself. She came to realize that she was a part of nature's grand scheme, not a rotten and unholy person who got cancer. Yes, her life was far too short, but still she lived and taught us to be strong but kind, truthful and curious, loving more than yourself.

I wrote this book as a memorial, of course, to her, and hopefully to give others a chance to appreciate the healing powers of art.

Part I

BARE TREES WITH THE
OPEN-BUD FULL MOON

When Amber died in the hospital, just short of thirteen years young, her lion's heart was beaten and her face became a death mask.

We watched her fight against the odds of surviving total-body radiation for almost a year. Later her mother, Kathy, would ask me time and again, "How did this happen? Especially in this hospital." All I could say was, "I don't believe it, she was so strong."

In the last few days of Amber's life (for this story, her nickname is Alee) she only whispered and barely opened her eyes. She was made more comfortable with the morphine drip, and never walked by herself again. The weekly doses of new blood and platelets were removed from her I.V. pole. She never asked for anything again-and passed into a deep sleep. All the doctors' recipes and transfusions couldn't heal her insides. The mucositis ran the whole length of her GI tract. She had coughed up blood on a daily basis. Kathy (from now on, she's called Lily) and Vera and Alee's father Jack never realized that she was dying right before our eyes. Slowly, every day for weeks, she began to fade-remembering less and less. And we prayed for a miracle.

When Alee stopped breathing in the early morning, after hanging on to her life for nearly four days, the *Mona Lisa* lost her smile, Montezuma cut our hearts out for sacrifice, and the blue sky never looked the same again. The wind was knocked right out of us—Vera and Jack shook their heads and went numb. Lily went into shock and couldn't cry or speak for days-as if she had gone with Alee to guide her up to heaven. We all wanted to go with her, but like the rhinestone-blue butterfly on her shirt, her spirit flew too fast and far away from this godless place. Wondering why her young life was taken before it ever happened, I glanced up at the night sky and saw Orion brightly rising. "That's where she is—located in Orion's nebula, beaming down at us." Like Leonardo created light out of a dark, primeval landscape, Mother Nature begins life anew; it grows in the sun and later becomes part of the cosmos. Life and death will come and go, but the spirit carries on. This was my mantra—believing science takes the body, but our energy goes back into a beautiful, vast, mysterious universe forever.

As Pieter Brueghel painted in 1560, in *The Fall of Icarus*, Icarus, who was the son of Daedalus, fails to listen to his father and flies too close to the sun. The wax on his wings melts and he falls into the ocean and drowns. The shepherd looks up, but never moves, he goes on tending his flock-dying becomes a part of the seasonal cycle.

It was about ten days after Alee died, when snow fell the hardest on record since 1969. Boston area schools were canceled and I found myself walking back over to the hospital, across the medical school yard, unable to stop swirling—like one of Van Gogh's exploding stars in *Starry Night*, 1889. As if in a tunnel, I made my way to the sixth floor, gravitating to the *Wall of Tears* photo collage. Amidst an array of circling faces, Alee's proud, smiling face, bareheaded and all, called out my name—I remembered her soft, weak voice saying, "Aunt Rosie...is it snowing outside? Go get me some snow, please." Before, of course, Alee hadn't been outside for months, and being immune-deficient, she was always "under precautions" I had hesitated for a second...looked at Lily's sad, watery eyes, and with a nod, I walked down to the garden courtyard. A raw, thick chill silenced the night, and as I scooped up some clean, white snow, light from the Hunter's full moon froze me like a corpse.

It hurt too much to deny Alee her simple requests. Especially since her eyes searched and begged for a way to escape her prison of pain. Walking out of the hospital would take a miracle, and she was beginning to give up. I will never forget the moment she put the snow on her lips to eat. We tried to stop her, like always, saying, "Your belly won't heal, honey...the doctors want only ice chips." She dreamed about food, asking for grapes, cherries, and a grapefruit sprinkled with powdered sugar. I prayed every day to see her eating again, but that day never came. Only once did she ask for french fries and coffee, and Lily replied, "How about a strawberry shortcake ice-cream? Here, hurry before the nurse comes in."

Alee took a couple of bites...and said, "You finish it, Mom, I can't." Lily found herself staring into Alee's bud-moon eyes—paralyzed by knowing everything she'll miss—when in marched the team of doctors. "We could try this for a few days...yes, let's wait and see what happens," said Doc Gily. I turned around quickly, thinking, *They don't have a clue...and then they make you sign all those consent forms with their trial and error procedures.*

Alee's hospital records and endless dosages of twenty different medications were kept daily by her mother—even the time taken and the amount. Lily was intent on having some control over this ordeal and parade of specialists. Her three—ring notebook was as thick as a dictionary. It was a masterpiece of organized documentation, and impressed all the experts who came to discuss Alee's treatments and "recipes." Lily had bound and created a grid-like plan of attack. Her hopes and fears for Alee's survival were kept inside-Alee never saw her mother cry or yell at the doctors. What we finally realized after six months was that Alee's pain and courage were never-ending. We never thought for a second that she was going to die. There were a few dim lights here and there, with Alee losing hope, but Lily was determined enough to keep her on a healing course of baby-steps, saying over and over, "Do this, it will make you better."

Living her last year in the hospital could not be the fate of a sixth grader; figure-skating, shooting stars…forget about her 20 percent chance. Like Mary, the Madonna, who calmly watches over the harbors and the faithful, Alee melted the hearts of everyone she met—looking out for her family and friends. Her high-spirited and daring personality made it easy to believe that she was capable of anything.

Eventually the final days arrived, though Alee still would not give up her strong hold on life. Weak and thin, with little or no muscle action, Alee would let the physical therapist work on her legs. One day Lily and I left the room for a few minutes. When we got back, the therapist said, "She asked me for a ride home…please, one time." It was as if she was echoing Dorothy's words, "There's no place like home." We knew then that Alee would never see home again, and she knew it too.

In the beginning of Alee's treatment, everything was still possible; even living happily ever after, like the fairy tale. She believed that taking all her medicines would make her normal again and help her get out of the hospital faster. All the cards, teddy bears, monkeys, jewelry, and visitors arrived one after the other. Her artwork and Beanie Babies decorated the room.

The first weeks were like walking through El Greco's expressionistic landscape, *The View of Toledo*. The tiniest people washing clothes by the river can be seen in the foreground. They are helpless and insignificant compared to nature's power. Then, climbing up the hillside through trees and shrubs to reach the protection of the church and city above, the people are hit by lightning. Anxious, scared, and dying, the innocent close their eyes against the darkening sky. Alee was in that landscape, shaking and searching for a way out, praying for new blood and hoping it was just a nightmare.

During the early months, movies were our salvation. Alee, Lily, Vera, and I would gather round the bed, eating teriyaki and nachos, while we talked and laughed through *Gone with the Wind* and *Casablanca*. We were watching the final scene in *Spartacus*, when Lavinia holds up their son-and the nurse came in with the mail. Lily was always getting letters from the various cancer foundations. They would send money and gift certificates to the most seriously cancer-stricken children. Alee said, "Let me see the cards." Lily handed her the mail and Alee asked, "What's Make-A-Wish?"

"It's a program for kids to go anywhere on vacation," said Vera.

"Where do you want to go?" Lily asked.

"I don't know, can everybody go too?" Alee inquired.

"Probably, but you have to write them a letter first and tell them your wish," Lily said.

Alee started to write her letter, then stopped and said, "What if I'm not here anymore?"

We all chimed in, "You will be, honey, don't worry."

This incident was long before the no-hair reality set in. The first chemo blast was nothing compared to what the doctors had planned for Alee.

Alee would have been a modern-day Helen of Troy—"the face that launched a thousand ships." Luminous, penetrating eyes, lips rosy and full, a small faintly freckled button nose. The most popular girl in her class, with *joie de vivre*...but in one year she looked like Frans Hals' *Regentesses*, with a worn-out, bloodless face of doom. I looked at her the day before she died, and shaking my head, getting angrier by the minute, I thought,

So they can kill all the mutant cells, along with the good ones, but not a bellyache?

All they could ever say was, "She was not healing fast enough and the bone marrow never started growing properly." From the very beginning, the prognosis was not promising—more like a fifty-fifty chance of survival. Of course Lily and Jack never believed anything but survival was in the cards. But the thought was always in the minds of the medical pros on the sixth floor. Somehow, looking back, I wish they had said, "This will most likely be Alee's last year."

Knowing the future, though, takes the joy out of the present. So unless Alee found the ankh, an Egyptian symbol for eternal life, she's living in the here and now; not preparing for her death, but planning for her homecoming.

Alee was truly uplifting to the other kids on the floor. I heard her talking in the art room one day to Lucy, a new, very scared twelve-year-old; "Yeah, it's pretty bad in here, everybody talks softly but carries a needle and syringe with them ready to get you."

"Hey, did the doctors say you were going to die?" asked Lucy.

"Oh no, but my Aunt Rosie told me about the talk the doctors had with my mom and dad," Alee replied. "She said they were crying, and my mom's head was down."

"Well, my mom said they have to kill the cancer before we can go home," Lucy replied.

"Yep. Gotta go," Alee replied. "See you later."

Alee grew up fast in that hospital room, lying in bed, trying to understand why her body got cancer and wanting desperately to believe that the chemo and medicine were going to kill it. Her eyes and ears never missed a trick or a whisper. Talking with her aunts about Nana and Papap, the Cottage Club, and nurses was a way for Alee to feel normal. She even laughed when her father got upset, saying, "Hey, that's not how it happened, and watch your language, cut the swearing and sex talk." Vera kept her smiling and got on a roll about the infamous "jello" fiasco and wet-T shirt contest. Alee was wide-eyed, but confessed, "Dad, I already heard about the naked dancing, Papap was telling his fishing buddies in the office."

Soon Alee was spending half a day in the art room. Sparkles, glue, and paper cut-outs were everywhere, while Alee sat helping the new kid on the ward. She searched for the saddest and most terrified face, then looked into their eyes, saying, "Don't be afraid, I'll help you." That was when Alee showed her true colors-truthful and fearless; she was a natural beauty, full of kindness and a wisdom beyond her years. Easy acceptance and indifference, she never understood; the purpose and meaning of her life came to light that day.

Lily kept a close watch on Alee's moods and mental state. She once said, "I feel like I'm dying, but never like I want to die." Often she woke up in pain with another bellyache or headache, and quickly Lily pressed her pain button and put a cold cloth on her forehead. The mouth sores were really bad, not even a popsicle made them better.

In the afternoons, Alee would hide out in the art room talking to Lucy and making shell paintings. It was best to sit and listen, instead of making small talk with her short, "no," "yes," "I don't know" answers.

Alee talked softly, asking Lucy, "When's the Make-A-Wish trip?"

"Don't know yet...hey, does it hurt to lose your hair?"

"No, not really, the worst part is seeing everyone come and go... smiling and talking about school. All I want is to go home too," Alee replied.

"Then what do you do all day?" Lucy asked.

"Well, I listen to my aunts laugh and tell stories, instead of all the doctors talk about bad blood," Alee replied. "Then I asked my mom and aunts to tell me about my Nana and Papap's restaurant," Alee continued. "Seems like a hundred years ago, but I used to run around with my sisters, helping Aunt Vera and eating little necks while my mom counted the money in the office. She would tell me to get down to the beach, but my grandfather would give us all a roll of quarters to play pinball. I was about eight years old but still had a cool time by the ocean." Alee sighed. "My Nana and Papap died a couple years ago, and summertime is totally different now."

Just then the nurse came rushing in, saying, "Hey, hurry up you two, it's time for doctor's rounds…and then you both need x-rays."

Lily and Jack always wondered how this could have happened to only one of their kids. Sitting off to the side when the team came around to see the patients, I heard the head doc say to Lily, "We all can possibly fall through the cracks. It only takes one cancer cell to start the ball rolling. It gets lost and masses together with others to multiply." Not the explanation any of us wanted to hear, nor could we understand, "They don't really know why one kid gets it, and the other siblings don't." Guess we needed a diagram…cause the medical jargon was just too complicated for us regular folk. The simple "cell falling through the cracks" was their standard explanation.

It would be a long time before we believed in their expertise. Not for saving the life of Alee, but for maintaining her bodily fluids and functions while she was alive. We were never told that Alee needed a miracle-only a stem cell operation. It's like the docs' textbook response; "We did everything we could, but sometimes the new cells take too long to grow…and get attacked by the Rota virus, or the host-graft skin disease." That was like having a third-degree burn all over the body. The little boy next to Alee often sat outside his room to eat and talk to the nurses-his rashy, bright red face was swollen and itchy. Seems half of the stem-cell transplant patients go through a semi-rejection phase after the procedure. Most come through it all right though, that is, unless they pick up an infection or virus beforehand.

Alee's lymphoma was aggressive and spreading. "That's where all the killer cells are located," Doc Gily said, "In the blood mostly." Every time the team came in to assess Alee, she only asked for one thing—not pain-killers, but "I need to go home now." She pleaded and begged with tears in her eyes. Of course, they couldn't say for sure, it was usually, "Let's see how the chemo goes first, maybe in a couple of weeks." The marked x's on the calendar went across the whole month, so Lily moved it out of Alee's sight.

Lily had to find out just when the disease started; was Alee born with it or was it from drinking all that contaminated water leaking out of the Air Base? She asked the social worker and doctors about the cancer clusters found in many Cape coastal towns. They told her to go on-line to register and research with the Disease Center for the northeastern area. That kind of information is available to anybody who wants to af-fix "charges" in a legal arena or join a class-action suit, but not common knowledge in general. It would take six months down the road for our inquiries to be heard by the regional health department-just another file on top of the stack. Decades of cancer studies have been done on Cape Cod water wells.

But Lily was totally focused on keeping Alee's spirits up. She handed all the paperwork and listings to me and Vera. Once a week we would make contact with other families and wage our outrage behind the scenes—against the carelessness of the military spills. Being put on hold for hours, e-mailing, and researching polluted water sites was a full-time job for a lawyer, and a class-action suit. Legal battles like that take time, which was running out for Alee.

Vera told me about the day when Alee came home from school dog-tired and barely able to walk. "Grab your skating bag, Alee, we have to go to the rink," her mother said. "You too, Jeanie and Annie."

Alee replied, "I can't, my legs are hurting."

"C'mon over here and lie down," Vera said. "Take your tights off."

Vera was shell-shocked, fighting back the tears, and whispered, "Oh my God, Alee...what did you bump into?"

"Nothing, why, Aunt Vera? We were running around the track during phys ed, that's all," she said.

Lily glanced over from the kitchen. "What's the matter?"

Vera imagined a head-on collision and crushed, bloody bodies...then Lily walked over. "Oh, it's all right, Lil, I'll stay here with her...she can't go skating right now," Vera announced. Looking at the swollen, purple-red bruises running up and down Alee's legs, Vera thought of her mother's medical book-ready to look up symptoms with bruises.

Alee was not moving, her eyes were closed, and her white skin was stained rose-red. Vera held her hand and softly said, "I love you, Alee."

Within minutes Lily called from the rink. "Vera, how is she?"

"Okay, I guess, but Lil, I'm really scared, she's all bruised up, and never fell down anywhere," Vera replied.

"Oh no, my God, what could it be?" Lily cried. "Should we go to the emergency—no, wait, Jack's home in an hour from work."

In a matter of days, Alee was taken from all she knew and loved. Her carefree, happy days were behind her now-an innocent girl just snatched up and away. As if Titian's *Rape of Europa* had come to life; Jupiter disguised as a white, cancer-demon bull comes prancing by the shore...then scoops up Europa for a ride, while her friends scream, "Come back!" She's carried off against her will to an island full of heartache.

Looking at art would become one of Alee's comforting distractions for the next year. Her curiosity was relentless; from Aunt Rosie's stories to the huge art text, full of colored reproductions and nudes. Seeing her great-papap's paintings hanging in the restaurant, dissecting his sketchbooks and postcards with Rosie and Vera had opened up a Pandora's box. "You know, Alee, it's easier to understand the pictures than read the words," Rosie explained.

"That's what happened to me at school," interrupted Alee, "I always looked around at everybody, instead of listening and reading."

"That can be good, honey, Leonardo says the eyes are the windows of the soul, and people's faces show their personality", Rosie said.

"What do you mean…the soul?" Alee questioned.

"It's like you can see a person's heart…and if they're kind, mean, lying, happy, or sad."

Childhood leukemia kills thousands a year, and there's no cure. For Alee it was the worst kind–AML or Acute Myelogenous Leukemia. This cancer of the blood and lymph nodes infiltrated the bones and vital organs in a few months. Her mind and body would never be free again. She might as well have been born a moonflower under glass. Nothing made sense anymore.

As Alee rested on the sofa, unable to walk, she closed her eyes, thinking it would go away…believing that by chance we are born and at random we will die-anytime and anywhere. Alee and Lily were told that only one hospital could help her fight this cancer-Children's Hospital. They all left for the city that night.

Alee had many calendars hanging in her sterile hospital room. The one for activities and events was supposed to keep the kids busy. She wouldn't get out of bed or talk to anyone for weeks after the first chemo treatment. "When will she stop fighting all of us, and realize she must take all this medicine," Lily wondered, "in order to live?"

It took weeks for Alee to turn the corner and walk around the ward. It began with the Russian folk singer and her guitar. Finally Alee had looked someone in the eye and said, "Where are you from?" Soon she was pushing her I.V. pole up and down the halls and then setting up shop in the art room. Dreamcatchers hung from the ceiling, sea glass was strung across the windows, and music played in the background. Alee, Mia, and Lucy chatted about movies and medicine, while they painted and decorated wooden boxes. Their sequined names sparkled on the top-it was Lily's most treasured keepsake, along with the one thousand origami cranes; symbolizing longevity. Alee was like a good-will ambassador-holding court and making frightened little kids forget about being sick. Not by talking, but by looking into their sad, scared eyes, holding hands, and playing picture games. Eventually her soft voice wrapped around them, and she hugged little Shannon Riley for weeks. Alee's instinctive way of coping with AML was to help the other kids take their medicine and see her smile. Her eyes were like a sky-blue heavenly cloud, carrying them away from all the pain, x-rays, blood transfusions, and bald heads.

As I walked past the activity room one day, whispering voices made me stop short. Lucy and Alee were sitting in the corner with their shirts pulled up, checking out their tiny, round breasts. Both were still virgins on the brink of puberty. A deep sense of loss welled up inside-I wondered about whether they would ever find true love, or hear a bobwhite or see the Grand Canyon. Tiny I.V. lines just below the heart area shot me back to reality. A small hole in the chest was a permanent reminder of the serious amount of meds needed to counterattack the multiplying mutant cells in the blood. Needle injections were rare at this stage. All the plasma, platelets, food, H_2O, chemo, anti-fungus, and painkillers went into their I.V. chest setup. Lily's daily med time chart dazzled the nurses. Alee's skinny body took in layers of chemicals that would have knocked out a grown woman for sure, but her big-heart serum was a powerful antidote.

On the same day, just down the hall, Lily and Jack sat in the family conference room with Docs Gily and Gardner. Lily's hands covered her face and she was rocking back and forth. Jack had his arms around her—she was crying out of control. The doctors gave them the worst news possible—Alee had a 30 percent chance of surviving this kind of childhood leukemia, or AML.

Better go find Alee…maybe we can work on the Celtic stained-glass poster, Rosie thought. *Anything to escape from the picture of Lily in the fetal position.* It was the only time Lily cried in front of the doctors-she was determined to beat this cancer down for her daughter.

When Alee and Lucy sat together, dark circles and hollow eyes stared back, their smooth-skinned heads stood out where long braids and pony-tails once hung.

Back in the art room, Rosie heard Alee loud and clear, "I threw up four times a day. When it was my birthday, I didn't even care…like I can eat cake and ice cream!"

"Yeah," replied Lucy. "My stomach hurts all the time, so I hate to eat."

"Well, my present is going home next week to play with my puppy, Cooper," Alee exclaimed.

"Hey, when are you going to Disney?" Lucy asked.

"Don't know yet, Make-A-Wish hasn't written back," replied Alee.

Alee had decided weeks ago that her "wish" trip would be to go with her brother, sisters, mom and dad, Aunt Rosie and Aunt Vera to Disney. Especially since she was planning to audition for the famous Cirque du Soleil theater group! When she first saw the Dralion show back when she was nine years old, sitting in the balcony she announced to us all that she was going to be an acrobat too. Alee was always jumping, dancing, and singing; following the yellow brick road. "And we're off to see the wizard…" If only one of her doctors had been a wizard with the magic touch and chemo recipe. Alee saw the Cirque as a place where she could be free to touch the stars. All her young life, she had skated effortlessly and somersaulted in gymnastics fearlessly. This looked like home to her.

One afternoon while I was sitting next to the bed knitting, Alee was particularly restless and couldn't get comfortable. There were more visitors than usual. Her grandparents from the Chicago area came to stay for a while. Alee never talked much in the last few months. Helpless and body-weary, unable to eat, she listened to Willy Wonka's chocolate factory music playing over and over in the background. Then she refused for the ninth time to take her morning meds. If it wasn't the nurses begging her, it was Lily coaxing her heart out; "Please, honey, it will help your belly."

All of a sudden, I glanced over and saw how Alee's head and body aches overwhelmed her. Tears soaked her face. Shaking and holding her swollen belly, she cried, "I feel like I'm dying." Lily looked at me in a panic, rang for the nurse, and grabbed another hot pack. "Alee, no, sweetheart, it's just a headache, let's take some Tylenol and put this on your stomach."

Lily had come to a turning point-that Alee probably knew she was dying...especially the time she vomited up tiny bits of bloody tissue from the linings of her stomach! After that episode, the docs upped her blood and fungus meds, along with adding strong sedatives and anti-seizure and anxiety drugs to keep her calm and help her sleep longer.

Lily was like that huge claw-like wave in Hokusai's print. Rising high and mighty, crashing down on all the suffering and pain-trying to save a drowning Alee. She was a powerful force of enveloping love. Living with Alee in the hospital for almost a year was a natural instinct for Lily. A mother's love can keep a child alive, as long as the body holds out. And Alee was far too sick to go home, so Lily moved right in next to her-and she was never alone again.

Right before Halloween, sick or not, Alee's wish-"Please, I need to go home"—came true. Seeing her walk out of the hospital that day was like seeing a shooting star flash right over your head. It was a remote possibility that Alee would go home again. Her life was anything but normal. There she was though, out trick-or-treating with her brother and sisters, dressed as a scarecrow. She was even able to go to school to get the class picture taken; bright-eyed and bald, Alee sat smiling like she had just found a pearl in an oyster. Her photo was heartbreaking, haunting and wonderful all at the same time. Then there's her beautifully shaped head and a happy face-masking the deteriorating fungus spreading in her body. As if Alee's standing in that golden wheat field with black crows circling above, symbolizing an impending doom. There's a hot wind blowing in waves across the wheat, an empty road goes nowhere, and the sun is beating down—causing a massive headache. It was Van Gogh's last great work, before he shot himself in a fit of despair... *Crows Over the Wheat Field* in 1890. The gray storm clouds circling above expressed Vincent's inner turmoil and hopelessness.

Alee's visiting nurses came every afternoon to give her shots and intravenous meds. It was not long before the bruises reappeared on Alee's arms and legs. Reality set in, and the doctors called for the next stage of chemo treatments. Alee never dreamed of having to fight another army of body-eating cancer cells—starting all over again.

Surviving and recovering from a second round of total body radiation was next to impossible-but young bodies and hearts fight harder.

The news on Alee's blood count revealed that she had suffered a relapse. Her fate was sealed and Lily's heart went cold. Alee sat at the kitchen table with her two best friends, Emmie and Samantha, chit-chatting away. "Guess I'll miss school this year...the tutor will give me homework in the hospital," Alee stated.

Lily came down the stairs and said, "Alee, did you pack all the art stuff and beads?"

"Yeah, Mom, when are we leaving?" Alee asked.

"Dad's driving us in a couple minutes, say good-bye now," Lily replied.

"You better come up and see me," Alee told her friends, "but I probably won't be there long...we're getting ready for the transplant." Lily watched all three hug and kiss each other.

Innocence, happiness, and hope flew away that day, and Lily's picture of Alee walking down the driveway holding hands was her last unforgettable image of her daughter's love of life. Like Michelangelo's last *Pieta*, where a worn-out Mary holds up the dying body of Christ, a last ray of hope still alive, but falling back he becomes one with her, and dies. The universal image of love-mother and child as one together, in the beginning and in the end-melting into each other's arms.

Jack and Lily drove up to the hospital in a silent cauldron of fear and frustration. Alee and her little brother, six-year-old Cody Ben, sat in the back playing Game Boy and trivia. Both her sisters had been tested for the bone marrow transplant. Only Cody had come out as the perfect sibling match. Even Lily knew some time ago that, "They are the most alike...and the chances are one out of four." And when we got the kids together to tell them, Cody jumped up, yelling, "Is it me, is it me?" Finding a match so soon was a heaven-sent blessing for Alee–as close to a cure as it gets.

But Alee's immune system was non-existent; Cody was to undergo the procedure of removing his bone marrow cells within the week. Alee created a special *He Is My Hero* scrapbook for Cody—the brother who was going to save her life. All the time in the hospital, Alee kept saying, "Is he okay? Does it hurt? I don't want him in pain." Cody was never afraid of the blood–machines-he was brave for his sister.

Weeks before the local figure skating show, Alee was practicing her program, skating to the music, "You Are My Hero. There is no video of this dress rehearsal, but that was the last time she was ever on the ice. The next day Alee's tests were done-Lily and Jack were told to check back in to Children's Hospital. She never skated to "Hero" in her first solo performance, but Alee's friends and teachers at the club played the song in her absence. The arena was flooded with tears and applause. She was there flying over the ice with her hero Cody - then her spirit jumped and soared even farther away to her Ambrosialand, a fantastic, imaginary place that Alee mapped out for a school project last year.

The bone marrow transplant operation was not going to be aggressive enough for Alee's kind of blood myeloma. The team waited weeks for the chemo and radiation to finish their destructive job of killing her bone marrow cells. Finally, a month later, after Cody's blood had been through apheresis or separated into plasma and platelets, Doc Ava decided that a stem-cell transplant would be a faster, concentrated method for growing Alee's new marrow cells. With smiles all around and hopes galore, Alee underwent the complicated procedure. The blood transfer went into the omnipresent I.V. line and flowed directly into her arteries and veins-as easy as saying, "I love you."

Lily received daily reports from the morning team. Doc Gily constantly reminded Lily about the positive results expected with a perfect sibling match and a strong-willed, tenacious Alee. But it took twice as long as it should for the new male cells to appear. By this time the total body radiation and chemo treatments had turned the linings and tissues of the GI tract into a bloody, oozing body sore. An army of medications could not soothe and heal the weakened, delicate passages. Alee's bodily fluids were leaking from the stomach, intestines, and liver. Her feet, face, and belly were purple and swollen. Never did the possibility arise that Alee would die. She had everything going for her; family, youth, and confidence. She was going to "win the fight of her life." But the immune system needs to attack and multiply its forces for survival. Alee did not have an immune system, until the bone marrow could replenish itself-and Mother Nature was not in the mood to fight her infection. Cody's cells never reached maturity and her blood became muddy; quickly the Rota virus infiltrated. Like a supernova traveling across the night sky, leaving a trail of twinkling stars in its path, Alee's bright-eyed, quick-tongued, "Why this, what now, I can't do it anymore," was fading fast.

The resource room manager had come for a visit, bringing along one of the hospital's first photo-phone companions. Alee woke up now and was smiling when she heard a voice and saw Lucy's face on the tiny screen. Most of Alee's friends had ALL, not as life-threatening as AML.

They were located on the upper floors, not in the newly sterilized ward for the worst cases of childhood cancers. The new phone was shared by the kids and their parents. Alee got her own, and only used it for a few weeks. After a time, she lost interest and gave up talking. Though one time I heard her say, "I hate that nurse, and those doctors know I won't listen anymore." I glanced over and saw Lucy's bandana-wrapped head nodding back and forth on the picture phone. Alee knew she wasn't getting any better. The medicine tubes would pile up from morning to afternoon. And soon Lily stopped hounding Alee to take her meds on time, "To get better."

It was a reckoning for us all to realize that Alee was as sick as ever, worn-out and needing too much new blood and platelets almost every other day. Alee had turned the corner; keeping her eyes closed most of the time, she started looking back towards her Lake Metallic, seeking those Goldeanna Caves in Ambrosialand. She dreamed about running up and down Lola's Vineyard—not red and fuzzy faces-riding her Pegasus across Diana's desert towards the seaside caves, far away from her hospital hell.

Alee's map of Ambrosialand was the first coincidence in a long line of many fateful events. Especially when she found her Papap's torn-up "treasure map" of southern Florida and the Bahamas. She was about nine years old, playing up on the third floor of the Cottage Club, just hanging out with her aunts, Rosie and Vera. They always took a break, drinking ice tea and napping up in their grandfather's attic studio, hoping to get a second wind before the dinner set-up. Rosie and Vera worked double shifts in the restaurant during the busy summer weekends. And then the attic even turned into their after-hours down-time spot. That is, if nobody made plans for a Trivial Pursuit game, because then it was a big time with beers, vino, pot, and lines until daybreak.

The Captain's studio was the best hideaway, but the smell of oil paint and linseed varnish still lingered. The discovery of our artist-grandfather's postcards, sketches, and photos revealed another time and place.

And it looked like his life and art had become one. Like Alee's other world, the map she found stuck to a box lid was colorful but ominous. Scratched dates, blue seas with floating glass buoys looked like one island fantasy along with a strange mix of amoeba-like creatures skimming the surface. Though not with trees, like Oz; more a place where angels fly and mermaids swim freely catching sharks. Where magic stars and fairy dust calm down the tragic, stormy seas of the Atlantic, while sea hawks nose-dive for fish parts, a lighthouse booms long and deafeningly, warning all of the treacherous, deadly possibilities up ahead. We tried to make light of the Captain's treasure map, but Alee wouldn't let it go.

Part II

THE STRAWBERRY OR FLOWER FULL MOON

The driftwood wall hanging, full of sea glass, jingle shells, and worm-eaten pebbles, was Alee's constant reminder of her days playing at the beach. Every morning in the summer and fall, at the family's Cottage Club restaurant, her mother sorted cash receipts and counted bags of money. All Lily's kids grew up there, with Papap carrying them through the restaurant and out onto the jetty. He came up into the office one morning all bloody at the knees. "Damn it, Lily, that Cody won't listen to me anymore. He ran out onto the rocks alone, and I fell trying to grab him."

"Okay, Dad, I'll take him home soon," Lily replied. "Alee, go get your brother, and don't run barefoot through the restaurant."

Even when Alee was a baby, smelling the seaweed as the gulls squawked overhead, crawling on the rocks was her favorite place. She was like a tiny sea turtle making her way through the sand to the water's edge. If only it was that easy to be free…to be saved from the random clutches of death. But it picks you out of a crowd. Even a dive-bomber's quick kill or high tide carrying the turtle too far from the shore and drowning is a blessing, from a seagull's sharp claws or cancer's vice-grip.

Alee's days in the sun were spent jumping over the hot sandy beach to the porch. Being swallowed up by the sea, running up the stairs to the deck, where the lunch crowd sucked down steamers, she'd skip through the restaurant, dripping wet, sandy toes and all, as if the days would never end-but that was a lifetime ago.

It was late August, after a four-month quarantine, when Alee opened her eyes and saw the jingle-shells hanging in the hospital room's window. She woke us up too, exclaiming, "Hey, remember when I found you guys up in the attic, hiding in the walls?"

"Oh yeah," said Vera, "but we were looking for the Captain's stuff, not hiding."

"That place smelled like gasoline," Alee said.

"Well, it was an art studio about a hundred years ago," Rosie replied.

"I heard you and Aunt Rosie yelling for help from the boardwalk," Alee insisted.

"You know what happened, Rosie was banging on the wall and the boards came loose and smacked her on the head," Vera said. "When we heard you running up the stairs yelling, we hid inside the wall."

"Why did you do that?" Alee asked.

"We wanted to scare you, but there was so much dirt and cobwebs, that we started screaming ourselves. You stood at the door, Alee, like a little monkey, jumping up and down laughing with those moon eyes," Vera said.

"What did you ever do with all those boxes full of pictures?" asked Alee. "And where's Great-Papap's sketchbook?"

"Oh yeah, those are his drawings of shipwrecks in the Caribbean. What do you think Tubby Dunbar was doing there?" Vera blurted out.

"Who's Tubby Dunbar?" Alee asked.

"The Captain's partner," said Rosie. "Saw him heading to the Everglades a couple of years back, Vera...and then a week later he was in Key West, fishing off the beach. He mumbled something about a lot of scavengers here, all except the Captain-he was the master."

Alee was downing the first set of morning meds, when she grabbed Vera's arm. "Auntie, what did he do, what happened?"

"You mean when he almost killed the Captain?" Vera asked. "Rosie's the one who hung around up there in his studio. I was only a teenager then."

"He got in deep, that's for sure," replied Rosie. "They couldn't prove that Captain Merri was part of the crew."

Alee had always wondered about her great-papap's portrait hanging in the solarium at the restaurant, looking out to sea. With her aunts Rosie and Vera hunched together and whispering up in the attic studio, she knew that something bad had happened. It was like the time she got stung by a man-o'-war. That jellyfish bite was as painful as all her leg—bone shots put together. And she just got stung for no good reason. "Why me?" she screamed over and over. "Honey, it's just bad luck, an accident," her mother said. *But it wasn't an accident,* Alee thought, *when the Captain hid all his postcards-maybe he was saving them for somebody. . .or keeping a secret.*

The branches of the family tree were more like the veins seen on a bolt of lightning; they were jagged and sparked out of control. The Merrick clan were the descendants of those medieval barbarian tribes roaming around Europe. The Celts, Franks, and Anglo-Saxons ruled and conquered northern Europe, along with the Vikings. The most feared and ruthless were the Huns, thundering across the Russian steppes, cutting off heads at every turn. In contrast to their brutality, the metal objects, jewelry, and illuminated manuscripts they produced are exquisite and ravishing-complex artworks created by the most violent cultures that ever lived. Like the Sutton Hoo ivory-enameled purse cover, and even the Ardagh Chalice, which have intricate abstract interlace designs and expressionistic animals devouring men. Even today, towns and cities have neighborhoods full of wanderers, misfit gangs, and criminals—like in the Captain's Pennsylvania hill-town.

The mentality of the Merrick family was work hard in the coal mines to put food on the table or die trying. Alee only half-listened to Rosie's history stories; explanations about ancestors from the 800s were incomprehensible—all she heard was that the family was a total mixed bag of loose marbles. "Grocers, bogmen, conductors, forgerers, and fishermen," Rosie announced. "Not a bunch of insane criminals, but desperate and violent characters for sure."

The Captain's photos and postcards became her obsession and she kept us going with the what, why, where, and how questions all summer long—ending with, "That can't be true." Explaining why the sky is blue would have been easier. It was a school project for Alee to trace the family tree as far back as possible. All her great-aunts and uncles were called up for names and dates. Details and birthplaces came out and Alee's curiosity about Great-Papap started growing from a tiny acorn into a mighty oak with spreading branches and dark, deep roots. Her watercolor showing The Tree of Life was a traditional symbol of wisdom, life, and death—inspiring all kinds of artists-beginning with the Bible, and the Fall of Adam and Eve eating from the Tree of Knowledge...of good and evil. Nature's majestic, towering guardians of the earth keep us in our place-and in awe of her sublime beauty. Trees are a universal, all-encompassing metaphor of humankind's journey. Different species represent man's moods and symbolize the passing of time-with birth, growth, and decay. The ancient Sumerians, medieval artists, Durer, colonial Americans, Cole and Van Gogh all used animals and trees to illustrate our personalities, telling us right from wrong-displaying Nature's energy. Albrecht Durer was especially keen on disguised symbolism-his engraving of Adam and Eve, from the German Renaissance, has animals and birds expressing states of being or humors; the cat for choleric or anger, the ox for phlegmatic or lethargic, the elk for melancholic or sadness and the rabbit for sanguine or sensual.

Alee's gold-rush fever consumed us all. She freaked out when the cigar box she found was taped shut. Words like Havana, mild, mucho dinero came off along with the tape as Alee lifted the lid. It got stuck, caught the paper on top, and torn-up pieces fell at her feet.

"Hey Aunt Rosie, that looks like a map...with the ocean...wait, aren't sinking ships with a black cross of skull and crossbones symbols of death?" Alee asked.

"What?"

"That's what Aunt Vera told me."

Rosie, the teacher in the family, stood up as if she was diagramming on an invisible blackboard. "Well, Alee, there are dual meanings for nearly all objects and creatures. For example..." Rosie explained.

"Just tell her what the squiggly doodles on the map mean," interrupted Vera.

"Oh, yeah, and the rows of tiny vases are the golden treasures found, right?"

"Listen, you two," Rosie replied, "one time, the Captain told me that the Amelia kids and their mother were lost at sea and drowned. That the *Topaz* crew found their schooner crashed onto the rocks. He was back on the mainland, copying a Velasquez painting for Mr. Amelia. Nothing was found on board intact, and Mr. Amelia disappeared. Who knows what really happened. It could be in this case; dead men and maps do tell tales of here today, gone tomorrow," Rosie said.

It was Alee who began this runaway buggy ride over the sand dunes and through seaweed to the edge of the Atlantic. Vineyard Sound was a reflecting pool compared to the unexplained mysteries of hidden Florida inlets, thinking about the legends of the Bermuda Triangle storms at sea. Many disasters conjured up visions-like *The Raft of the Medusa* by the Romantic great, Theodore Gericault. Gericault paints how the survivors were drifting for weeks, without food and water, based on a true 1819 episode at sea. Naked and dying one by one, the Michelangelesque figures resorted to cannibalism in order to survive. The extreme chiaroscuro dramatizes the piled-up bodies, as the waving men struggle to alert a ship on the horizon.

Alee sat puzzled and worried; she looked at the raft with horror-realizing that in this world anything is possible, when it's a matter of life and death.

"Did they all die?" Alee cried.

"It looks like it, honey," Rosie replied, "but the story goes that the starving survivors were spotted by a trading ship and rescued. The shipwreck was one thing, but to drift for weeks on a raft led to cruel, inhuman acts. They were dying fast, and trying to survive, so they became cannibals."

The clean-up of the studio was more like fitting together a 500-piece jigsaw puzzle. Ragged, ripped-up sketches, torn postcards, and faded photos were all missing dates. Alee started looking at postage stamps, matching up colors. Her determination and imagination carried her through the mess—hour after hour. Rosie watched in awe, as she sorted and scotch-taped the piles of papers. *Weaving a summer and winter eight-harness double coverlet was a hop, skip, and a jump compared to the Captain's loose sketchbooks,* thought Rosie.

Vera told Alee to run downstairs and study Great-Grandpap's paintings in the restaurant. "Not now, gotta finish the pile of...hey, they're just pictures of people eating and drinking," Alee said. "Why do I have to see that again?"

"Look honey, your mom's wondering why you're not swimming and playing with Annie on the beach," Vera replied.

"Just go, Alee, and check out the details really close...think about the colors, you'll see more of the story," Rosie explained. "Yeah, the people are fat and ugly, but art is also about themes or ideas...and your emotional response to..."

"Okay Rosie, let her go now and find Lily," Vera interrupted.

Alee stomped down the stairs, yelling, "Be back soon!"

The seascapes and portraits hanging in the Cottage Club were the Captain's diary for the past sixty years. His caricature style was a social commentary on people, drunkenness, and the high seas, much like the English illustrations and paintings by the master, William Hogarth. *A Rake's Progress* was a four-part series about a wastrel, a partying scoundrel in 1732. The upper crust of London society was exposed by Hogarth for two-faced phonies and hypocrites, who married for money and titles. His political satire was right up the Captain's alley; drawings communicating the abundance of life and folly.

Captain Merri had his own *Martini Drinkers* series—an updated version of social degenerates-drunk and demoralized. Then his other side, the seascapes, were wild white-capped, blue-green Homeresque waves of "Don't mess with me." Rosie told Alee many times that his portraits were both humorous and sad, excited but unhappy people ready for a good time.

Alee wondered, "Why do they have big, red noses and droopy eyes? And smeared red lipstick?"

Vera grinned and said, "Well jeez, Alee, they've been drinking and smooching all night. You know the Captain lived in Key West most of the time..."

"He told me he worked on the *Topaz* with his partner, Tubby Dunbar," Rosie said. "His favorite bar was called the Blue Parrot, where he sat and drew portraits of the customers. Looks like it was a pretty rowdy joint with all kinds of locals and hangers-on. Reminds me of Degas' *The Absinthe Drinker*...ex-cafe bourgeoisie types—lonely alcoholics, hooked on a crushing, addictive licorice liqueur. It also pushed Van Gogh over the edge, when he cut off his earlobe. And it didn't help his mental state at all when Gauguin went home that same night with his favorite prostitute."

"To me, Rose, he's more like the Moulin Rouge customers, painted by Toulouse-Lautrec," Vera announced. "Because the Captain's style is bold and colorful in the same way."

Alee, all ears and anxious, replied, "Show me in the art book what the people looked like so I can see who Great-Grandpap liked the best."

There was no way to feng shui the clean-up of the attic studio. Discovering the snippets of the fishing charters with the Captain and the *Topaz* crew was like following the ribbon-interlace on the Cross page of the *Book of Kells,* a famous Anglo-Saxon manuscript, c. 800. The curving designs were never-ending and interconnected to all the over and under layers of colored circles.

Vera glanced over at the bits and pieces of paper arranged on the floor by Alee and said, "Looks like Alee's making a landscape with trees or..."

"No, it's going to be a collage of Great-Grandpap's map pieces," Alee announced.

"You know, you draw pretty good...with a firecracker imagination, Alee," Rosie commented. "Let's put the sketches back together in chronological order...and make sure that rock of Sisyphus doesn't roll back down on us..."

"What are you talking about?" asked Vera.

"Just that it looks like our Papap did more than just copy the masters and caricature tourists. The map shows that the crew was busy giving sport-fishing charters. The x's and o's are too close to the shore and in the coves for fishing." Rosie summarized. "Looks more like places to get rid of stuff..."

"Look, Rosie, can't we go through the Captain's notebooks with the doodles and check them with the postmarks?" Vera wondered. "Maybe Mom and Dad would tell us about Key West."

"You mean about the time when they went to the Keys to see him?" inquired Rosie. "Bet they don't want to talk about it...or face the truth. When Papap came here to live, he had all kinds of people looking for him. Mom was not happy about it, but Dad kept saying, 'What can I do, he's my father!' Really though, it was wonderful to have Papap here...and he was an artist!"exclaimed Rosie. "Following him from the deck to the beach carrying paint tubes was special...and Papap was old then, so he couldn't do everything. He sat in the studio sometimes, next to the window, with paint-filled jelly jars lined up like a rainbow, sweeping his paintbrush across the paper, outlining circles and ovals. Then, like magic, grimacing faces and bulging red eyes appeared. And he always painted fat people walking down the boardwalk in skinny bathing suits," Rosie chuckled. "It really was funny and sad at the same time. Especially the women, like Toulouse-Lautrec's dancing Jane Avril meets de Kooning's *Woman I*-clashing black and orange colors symbolized the depraved Parisian nightlife, while slashing, broad brushstrokes create a voluptuous and vulgar earth goddess like de Kooning's."

"Remember when you brought that fifty-pound textbook to show Alee all the famous paintings…and all she wanted to look at was the nudes?" Vera asked.

"Yeah, and Lily thought it would give her ideas," replied Rosie.

"Alee just simply announced that everybody at school already knew about sex and boys" laughed Vera.

The hot and humid afternoons, up on the third floor, never bothered Alee. She left often to go jump in the ocean. On the way back up she'd grab a couple of stuffies for us. Alee was determined to put together her great-grandpap's faded drawings. One day she exclaimed, "This is like making a mosaic in pottery class…but now the faces look familiar, like maybe they were his friends."

The box of old photos and postcards had set in motion an avalanche of rolling sea pebbles, tumbling into a stone wall. It was nearing Labor Day when the studio was transformed into a wall of colored, shifting patterns. Vera tacked up white poster board, as if in a classroom, making the Captain's tiny sketches spring back to life. Alee and Rosie pasted together the drawings on the left side, while Vera glued photos and postcards on the other side. Rosie stood up next to the various sections of the composition to explain, "This is the best way to make a comparison…first, Vera, start taking notes about the map dates and postmarks. Alee, put dates on the sketches starting with…"

"Slow down," Vera ordered, "it's getting late. Alee has to go anyway, 'cause Lily's finished for the day."

"We're at a crucial moment here, Vera," Rosie stated. "If we can compare and match up the…"

"Okay then," Vera interrupted. "Alee, go get us a couple of ice teas, it's hotter than a witch's tit up here."

"Not now, Aunt Vera, let's see about the…" Alee said.

"Go ahead, Alee, we'll figure it out later," Vera promised.

Alee scooted out lickety-split, barreling down the stairs. Vera quickly turned to Rosie and said, "Are you sure Alee can hear all this stuff about Papap…especially the map, Rosie, there's shaky goings-on with that *Topaz* crew and Tubby Dunbar."

"I know, and it's probably true-those symbols on the map look very suspicious, like grave markers," replied Rosie.

"Alee's pretty cool, she won't tell, if we make her…think this could be why Papap came back here?" Vera asked. "To escape?"

"Be careful, we could start a lot of trouble here," Rosie replied.

Lily's voice called from the boardwalk, "Hey, Vera, gotta go to the bank."

In a flash, Vera stuck her head out the window. "Okay, where's Alee?"

"She's staying with you guys be back in an hour or so," Lily replied.

Alee came rushing into the studio. "Are you ready?"

"Alee, this is pretty serious. If we discover that the Captain knew people were dying or something, nobody can find out," whispered Vera.

"For crissake Vera, it's not that bad. Don't scare her about that," warned Rosie. "Look, Alee, whatever we find out is only a coincidence….okay? We're just guessing anyway, so don't let your imagination go hog wild."

"Don't worry, I won't tell anybody," announced Alee. "Let's just look at the map and check off the names…"

"Vera, are you ready to write down any similarities with the sketches and dates?" Rosie asked. "Alee, if the faces look familiar on the photos, stop right away. It's possible they were the customers on the *Topaz*. The Captain made money by drawing tourists, right? Maybe he used photos too. Most of the twentieth-century artists were influenced by photography."

Like the surface of a pond when a pebble skips over it, the ripples add up to a wave. As Alee unfolded the map of faded island haunts, she imagined sunken treasure and her great-papap's paintings covered with barnacles and starfish. Her mind was rolling in and out with the tide, begging us to find out about the black arrows on the map-the comings and goings of the *Topaz*. At times her face lit up the studio like a jack-o'-lantern, other times her dead silence put us all in a mood of drop-jawed disbelief.

The sketchbook and old photos revealed an underwater, shadowy world of blurry forms and faces, images performing a ghost dance for Alee, highlighted by streaks of sunslivers breaking the surface and penetrating the depths. All was changing and becoming something else-organic abstractions in a Joan Miro painting. His creatures are shifting, colorful dancing insects or body parts-as if Alee's free-wheeling, imaginary Ambrosialand turns into Miro's *Carnival*.

Explaining to Alee about the possible reasons why the Captain turned his love of art into a hit-and-run scam would be a hell of a lot easier than figuring out why someone gets cancer. How Alee got AML instead of the less-fatal ALL. Why she had to die and some other AML children lived. As if fate, science, and luck are the gods that rule over us, the here and now sets up the obstacles for us to overcome or break us down. Even the great artists, who paint their philosophies of life, knew that the past prepares us for understanding the present, why we're here on earth. Like Gauguin's masterpiece of 1896, on the cycle of birth, life, and death-*D'ou venons-nous? Que sommes-nous? Ou allons-nous?* (Where do we come from? What are we? Where are we going?)—the meaning of our existence was a mysterious and complex riddle for Gauguin-until his dying day. Soon after he tried to commit suicide on the beach, swallowing arsenic, eventually he died in his hut suffering from syphilis instead. The islands of the "noble savage" were not pure and innocent, as he thought, but already exposed to Western ways by Cook's expeditions.

Alee's death was tragic beyond belief. Her short life was more like a chrysalis which quickly transforms into a butterfly. Tigerlily was the nickname Rosie and Vera gave her that summer—in the search for Great-Grandpap's bag of sharks' teeth. *Maybe if she didn't find the map, he could have rested in peace,* thought Rosie. Her mind was flashing and her eyes were twinkling like stars in the night sky. Alee even sketched a tiny picture of Florida and the islands on the poster board, floating in a turquoise sea. She announced to Vera one day, "Look, now we can mark the spots where the boats sunk."

"It's not the boats, Alee," Vera replied. "It's what the crew put in those places that we need to figure out."

"Yeah, the shipwrecks have an x on them....but the o's are something else, it stinks of......well, don't really know," Rosie admitted.

The journey of discovery slowly sailed them through uncharted waters. Moving across the Atlantic, the Captain headed for Europe, while Dunbar and the crew maneuvered around the Keys. Especially challenging were the postcards from famous museums; just signed "Bull" and addressed to "*Topaz.*" Alee often got distracted and screamed, "These are the same paintings from the text! Look and see the..."

"Slow down, honey, we know," Rosie whispered. "Show me later, do you see any names or places of..."

"Where's the Prado? I think it has the *Garden of Delights* and the Louvre has the *Mona Lisa*...right?" Alee inquired. "It's on the postcard."

"Good, now go get your art book," Rosie instructed. "Let's double-check."

"Try to find the pages with the paintings on the postcard," said Vera, "and star the sketches that match up. You know, understanding art is easier than you think...easier than figuring out the Captain's zig-zags. Art is like traveling through time, seeing what was true and beautiful, through the artists' eyes. It makes you think, laugh, and cry-even musicians, dancers, and actors have the power to hypnotize us. The aesthetic experience is very personal and communicates all aspects of human nature-mostly it tells a story...teaching us about good and bad..."

"Wait, Rosie, let's get back to why the Captain chose those pictures to send back from all the museums," Vera insisted.

"Okay, just remember that art can be like people; mysterious. It can play tricks on the eye and have secret symbols. Papap probably drew and greatly admired those masters...fulfilling his dream to go see the originals."

"Alee, sort the cards into portraits, landscapes, religious and genre subjects first...maybe there's a connection," Rosie explained.

Whenever Alee flipped through her art book, she always stopped and stared at Botticelli's *Birth of Venus*. But it was the *Primavera*, or Birth of Spring, looking like a mille-fleur tapestry, that reminded Rosie of Alee. In the center, an earthly Venus suggests the Virgin Mary, and blesses the Birth of Spring. Flora's on the left, next to Chloris, who's being pursued by the wind god, Zephyr. It's one of the most complex, Christianized-mythological allegories ever painted. Alee stands in as a modern-day Venus-pure and sacred.

The masterpiece was the companion to *The Birth of Venus*—painted for the Medici Palazzo, about 1482. It was the flawless beauty of his female figures that stopped time. Flora alights onto a blanket of wildflowers, while the three graces dance together in poetic flight. Alee sat in wonder, looking at the painting, while Rosie told her the story: "It's based on Neo-Platonic ideas-Venus symbolizes Mary...pagan myths combined with Christian stories. People discussed it during the Italian Renaissance, Alee...just think of her as a symbol of goodness. She's goddess of earthly and divine love; on the left, Mercury in pink banishes the clouds away with his staff, while on the right, the blue god kidnaps the nymph, Chloris. But she escapes by turning into Flora, clothed in a flower dress. In the center, a Madonna—like Venus stands under an arch-like halo, while a blind Cupid above aims his flaming arrow at the three graces, who symbolize three phases of love."

Alee possessed the same fleeting charms of beauty, brightness, and joy, Rosie thought. The delicate, ephemeral figures expressing both the physical and divine female spirit. As death devoured Alee's body, she was reborn again as Flora. Art imitates life at any time; our place in the world is a never-ending cycle like the seasons born again. Alee is forever young, coming in and out of our lives-a guardian over truth and our lobster-claw of courage. Whenever we need to be strong and remember nature's wondrous beauty-she's tapping our shoulder with a cool breeze rustling the leaves.

Analyzing the scribbles and writing on the map required a magnifying glass and palette knife. Rosie lightly scraped off glue and scotch tape to uncover a name, "Captain Merri," in the lower right-hand corner. Light had faded the watercolors, but scattered islands and rock piles were still visible. Rows of purple and gold vases with numbers scrawled alongside them floated on a pale blue sea.

Alee sat cross-legged, shaking her head. "Aunt Vera, this is confusing...wasn't Great-Grandpap in the museums most of the time?"

"Maybe we should take a break...and go for a swim to wake up," Vera replied.

Rosie glanced up from her cat-nap and said, "Try to get the dates of the postcards in order, Alee, we can match them up with the *Topaz* trips. We'll figure out when he was away."

Only the Captain and Tubby Dunbar knew what the map was used for, and probably the Captain painted it as a record of sorts, thought Rosie.

All the postcards ever said was, "Weathering the storm, send some oils, see you in a fortnight, Merri," followed by his seagulls' V sign.

"Hey, Aunt Rosie, the only thing to do in a museum is to look at the artwork, right?" asked Alee.

"Maybe for us little people, but not for the artist," replied Rosie. "It's an education for them...studying the great masters' techniques. All the Realists in the nineteenth century set up their easels in the Louvre, and copied for hours. It was part of their training, besides painting in the studio of a master or in the Academy Julien. Even today it's the only way to study traditional style aspects. But then there was the avant-garde; innovators and radicals, who painted from their imagination or plein air."

Vera interrupted the art history lesson and told Alee to go downstairs and grab some chowder. "Don't forget the oyster crackers, honey...and spoons," Vera hollered. "Rosie, try to find out what famous paintings the Captain was studying."

"You mean copying, right?" Rosie snapped back. "Why would he write to Tubby for more oils and brushes?"

"But why would he be copying the Old Masters, anyway? He was old enough to know all their techniques," wondered Vera.

Alee was back in a flash with plastic cups of clam chowder. "Ready to finish the match-ups?" she asked.

"Almost, Alee, bring the art text over here first..." She dropped it hard on the table with a thud loud enough to crack marble. "Look up the Bosch triptych first, at the Prado."

"Well, it's good to know what he was copying...but better to know why," Rosie announced, "and what could have happened to them."

"Hurry up and tell me what's next...gotta go to the rink soon," Alee begged. "Mom's almost done in the office."

"Just get going, Alee," Vera ordered.

"We can't hurry up here...Great-Grandpap visited too many museums, and not for the fun of it. Somebody was sending him money to travel around and paint 'cause he was in touch with the *Topaz* crew," Rosie insisted.

Lily suddenly yelled up the stairs, "Alee, it's time for your lesson, hurry."

It was only a matter of time before Alee found out that her great-grandpap was more than the roly-poly artist in the red beret that his self-portraits suggested. Mostly he painted himself in the backgrounds, wearing a paint-stained royal blue T-shirt, with a brass whistle hanging on a macramé rope around his neck. He looked like a goateed wizard sitting on the pier at sunset down in the Keys-unkempt and bohemian for sure, but not the starving, temperamental type.

Bull "Captain" Merrick had more than skeletons in his closet-crumpled up family letters and photos from the '20s revealed a tough love/hate relationship with his father. When Bull, the youngest son, left to join the merchant marines, he broke his parents' hearts for good.

The Merrick clan were the town bullies—coal miners from Mt. Carmel. One brother played football in high school, another one was a fireman from the hose house two were miners, like the old man, and Bull was a sailor. His only sister Mary embroidered and sewed church vestments.

The Merricks were considered confrontational and vulgar. They worked day and night, but lived and drank even harder.

A Margaret Kurtz married a Joseph Merrick sometime around 1900, after they arrived in New York City. The Captain didn't know when they settled outside of Philadelphia. He told Rosie that's when he got a beating for drawing eagles on his blue bedroom walls. No one had any money really, the neighbors were poor and always fighting and the young kids hung out at the corner variety store looking for butts.

The Captain had a reputation for skipping school and jumping the trains. The railroad tracks ran just behind the black creek in the backyard of their three-decker. His father, "Bull" Merrick Sr., was hard as nails, a head-butter, picking fights and working the rails; that's how he got his nickname. He worked on the caboose after he came up from the coal mines all day "On the weekends he took me on the back of the caboose," the Captain said, " 'Watch out, we're moving fast, people coming and going all the time here, son...this is better than any schooling, right?' That's what my old man used to say. Guess it just came natural, to draw a bit of the towns and people hurrying along...been traveling ever since-started out as a sailor."

Papap saved a couple of silver crosses and frayed news clippings in the shoebox, along with photos of his sailor-friends. One headline said it was a rescue mission—"Sailors Lost at Sea"-his crosses were for bravery. Soon thereafter the Captain got his honorable discharge. He stopped sketching whenever he told Rosie about circling sharks and body parts. The missing and the dead crew members were his shipmates and buddies. "Did he go home after that?" Alee inquired.

"Yeah, to see his kids and mother...but not to welcoming open arms," Rosie replied. "It reminds me of Rembrandt's *Return of the Prodigal Son.* Look it up, Alee. But it was different returning home for Great-Grandpap...his father had died. Rembrandt's painting shows a father's love and forgiveness for the black sheep who wasted his money and time..."

"What's a black sheep?" Alee asked.

"Someone who disobeys their parents, and does everything wrong," Vera stated. "It's a Bible story, honey, about family love and loyalty."

"Asked him about Nana once," said Rosie. "Guess his Bridget left for Ireland with little Francis, and the oldest boys worked in the mines for a while...then he clammed up...wiping off his brush and eyes.

Then he said 'it was better to live alone on an island, than to feel guilty and lost at home'...sent some sketch money to help but never really saw them again."

His only family was Tubby Dunbar and the *Topaz* crew. Probably the motley cast of characters in his paintings were part family as well, since many of them looked like drunken sailors and old babes. His own family, Rosie remembered, were never in his paintings. It was a painful subject leaving his wife and boys to go out to sea. This was the part about Great-Grandpap that Alee didn't understand, which was fine with Rosie and Vera. He cast his spell over her with his paintings and that's just what he wanted to do anyway.

"Sometimes the Captain talked while painting his murals…he said he lost heart, and the only salvation was to travel around and paint people," Rosie said. "Sometimes you really can't go home again, and forget everything."

The Captain's driftwood plaque, painted in black, said it all too well, "Pride is good, pride is strong, pride endures when love is gone." Rosie never figured it out entirely, until the one time when the Captain said, "Yeah, escape into the Old Masters." She knew about the famous artists, especially the ones the Captain admired. The postcards framing his studio window were from the Prado, the Louvre, the Vatican, and London's National Gallery-art by Raphael, Titian, Rubens, Hals, and Velasquez. But being hand picked by the Captain to copy meant something else altogether.

The white poster board was now an enormous collage. Not a synthetic Cubist one by Picasso, more like a Dadaist's photo-montage by Hannah Hoch, full of pasted pictures within pictures, revealing hidden messages ambiguously combined with cut-up faces and lettering. Alee stood in front, touching up the blue-green sea and islands with colored pastel sticks. Her shiny stickers of ladybugs, seahorses, and dragonflies sparkled here and there. She beamed back at them with a proud glorious flower-face that would have knocked the socks off Georgia O'Keeffe herself.

We bragged and admired our handiwork for hours; it was a visual puzzle of sea life and whodunit. Alee kept up her curious, wide-eyed, reach-for-the-stars dance going…all she wanted to imagine was that the

Captain and the crew were searching for underwater treasures. Even Tubby Dunbar, his best buddy, had said, "We're all scavengers down here, rustling up business for the amateur mucky-mucks to go out tuna fishing and deep sea-diving-it was like picking teeth!"

Indian summer by the sea had wrapped around us like a Navajo eye-dazzler blanket. Nature was resplendent in all its regalia. The Hunter's or Falling Leaves full moon at the end of October was a golden ball of orange on the rise; summer folk had long since departed back over the bridge. Alee had gone into the sixth grade that fall, and Rosie returned to the city. On the weekends we got together to finalize our attack on the *Topaz*.

The Cottage Club would be locked up tight by Thanksgiving. The pounding waves and whitecaps were a constant reminder of the dampness and cold weather ahead. Vineyard Sound was now steel-gray, with a ferry crossing here and there. Off-season was a time for ocean reflections, seaweed piles, and collecting jingle shells.

Vera and her dad, or the Baron, as he was called, still worked every day packing leftover inventory away for next spring. On Halloween weekend a final monster bash had been set up, with spooky ghosts and skeletons lurking in the corners. Jack-o'-lanterns were hanging from the ceiling, flickering here and there. The whole family and the local townspeople were rocking and rolling to Beaver Brown. On that Saturday morning, Alee, Vera, and Rosie toasted their last good-bye to the Captain's map and paintings. The new "master switch" collage was still hanging up when Rosie turned around; "Looks like it's time to make a trip south...and find Tubby Dunbar."

"How are you going to do that?" Alee asked.

"Have to wait till school vacation," answered Rosie.

"Why don't we do it when we're all at Disney, in January," Vera suggested.

" 'Cause the Disney trip is a family vacation...just for fun and Mickey," Rosie replied. "Trying to find anybody left from the *Topaz* crew will be trouble enough."

"Did we figure out the whereabouts of Papap yet during the same time the crew was out fishing?" Alee's head jerked around. "Hey, he was in the museums painting his favorite artists, remember...they were his best friends. Vera, check out the postmarks again...the cards were sent during the summertime, right? And...it was all the time," Alee announced.

"We already did a cross-check," replied Vera. "Yes, he was at the Louvre and the Prado then. Working on the Velasquez, Degas's *Dancer*, and Titian's portrait...he was busy, all right."

"Maybe he had to copy them for somebody?" asked Alee.

"Why would you say that?" Rosie wondered. "He could have been alone."

"You said he needed money and paints...and yeah," interrupted Vera, "he stayed in some fancy hotels...friends of Tubby Dunbar."

Sitting in silence for the first time, Alee looked scared. Rosie and Vera saw a band of criminals taking rich people for a ride and forging artworks on the side. The Captain was the master-switchman, in a performance worthy of an academy award. Alee broke the spell: "Aunt Rosie, was Great-Papap playing a game?"

"No, it was a big-time fraud," said Vera. "Art forgery means jail-time."

"Hold on," Rosie quickly responded, "don't say that, Vera...that's serious stuff, especially when we can't really prove it."

"Why, what's wrong with that?" Alee inquired. "It's not like they were killing anybody. Just fishing and going to museums, right?"

"Well, going down to Key West could help...we already know that the Captain was copying in the Prado from the postcard-same time as the *Topaz* accident in the Bahamas," stated Rosie. "There has to be a connection."

The intermingling between art and life was like the sun and the moon during an eclipse—covering up with shadows, both changing and becoming each other over time. Imagine Hokusai's colored woodblock print of *The Wave*; looming and threatening, ready to engulf the tiny men shaking in the skiff. In the background is one of nature's wonders, Mt. Fuji, with its perfect vanilla-ice-cream-cone top. The sea gives and it takes lives. The jagged whitecaps contrast with the majestic order and serenity of the mountain and the Old Masters. Art pitted against the life-force of the punishing, random destruction of the sea-like the *Topaz* crew's fraud and deceit, while the Captain got caught up in the clutches of a scamming, mean-rotten-nasty ringleader called Tubby Dunbar.

Alee's innocence and curiosity would survive the discovery of the Captain's part in all the back-stabbing schemes. Following the trail of artworks became her own maiden voyage across the Atlantic. She paid no mind to stolen art and missing people. Alee was in dreamtime, riding in her Ambrosialand, nestled between the adventures of *Pirates of the Caribbean* and the Cottage Club by-the-sea.

Alee was a reflection of a Fra Fillippo Lippi Madonna. Her love of family and sacrifice of life were the true measure of humankind, and a reminder to us all of what was most important in the world. Sitting in the studio like the deaf, dumb, and blind monkey trio, Rosie and Vera pretended everything was hunky-dorey, until Alee exclaimed, "How did those people die on the *Topaz* anyway?"

"What? Oh Alee, nobody was ever found washed up on shore," Vera explained. "Maybe there were a few shipwrecks, but we don't know what happened. It does look pretty mysterious on the map...about T. Amelia."

Rosie stepped over to the collage and eyeballed Vera intently. "It says 'chartered 6/21/39—I not man overboard! They were fishing for marlin, not looking for bodies!"

"Yeah, and there's this postcard from the Prado dated 6/26/39," Alee answered. "It says, 'Velasquez—*Triumph of Bacchus and Musicians*, 1652. For T. Amelia, North Carolina-Flying Hill.' "

"That's what is so strange." Rosie pointed. "Here's the schooner, its masts down, near Nassau...see the tiny arrows...and the name on the side looks like *Airheart*...it could be his boat sunk there."

"Well, the Captain was probably painting for him...only something went wrong, a family accident at sea...or someone drowned," Vera stated. "There's old newspaper clippings mixed in with the photos, see this headline; 'Family Tragedy-Tycoon Vacationing in Spain.' "

Rosie remembered when her Papap first moved into the studio. Rumors were flying everywhere—about the *Topaz* charter expeditions and how the Captain was hiding out rather than rat on his buddies or go to jail. She heard her mom and dad arguing all the time. "It's not a good idea to harbor a fugitive." "He's my father, and not a criminal." Newsprint torn up in the cigar box was sent by Tubby Dunbar, from the local rag, the *Key West Banner*.

"Hey Vera, look in the sketchbooks...there should be more about the *Topaz*," ordered Rosie. "Papap never talked much-he came back here to live and be with family. He'd say...go on, doll, look at the sketchbooks and portraits."

Then a rude awakening occurred, when Rosie found the front page from November 10, 1948—"Stolen Art Turns Out To Be Fakes." It had been highlighted..."the F.B.I; searching for local fishermen connected to the sports-charter boat, the *Topaz*... T. Dunbar wanted for questioning...The Captain said it was all a mistake and 'all I ever did was paint for the tourists and the Old Masters.' "

"Don't worry, Alee, Great-Papap was an artist first and then a fisherman. He wasn't part of a gang of murderous thieves like..." Vera stopped short.

"No, nothing like that," interrupted Rosie. "He came back home to see his family...and nobody ever got arrested anyway."

Alee was smart enough to know the truth, but too young to comprehend the reasons why humans do what they do. Her imagination was already in overdrive, and the electricity between Rosie and Vera had sparks flying over the deadly business of the *Topaz* and art. They were bound together now, closing up the attic studio, folding up the map collage and hoping the Captain was just another one of T.D.'s innocent victims. Like winding a warp and tying it to the loom, the skeletal threads were ready for weaving in the weft. Alee wound the yarn into balls, Vera loaded up the shuttles, and Rosie threaded the heddles. It took a team effort to start the weaving process, just as the map collage required all their ideas for the final picture. Color and pattern will set the harnesses in motion-and little by little the whole story-design takes shape.

Alee was like a rare, pink lady's slipper—having a surprising and chance meeting with one is an unforgettable experience. Especially now, with her sense of belonging and love of family coming to light. Instead of giggling about boys with her girlfriends, she was flipping through the Captain's notebooks, alongside her art history text. It was late Indian summer, time for getting into warm jackets and mohair sweaters. Time for Alee to settle into the sixth grade.

Part III

The Falling Leaves or Hunter's Full Moon and Sky-Blue-Pink Sunsets

Rosie had gotten on her soapbox a few too many times for Vera's liking. As too much laughter leads to crying, her old master lectures put Vera over the top and she lost her temper. Rosie started telling Alee about the great Royal Collection at the Prado in Madrid. They had been talking about Goya's etching, *The Sleep of Reason Produces Monsters,* about all the symbolism in the cat and bats flying over his head. The etching suggests that Goya's dark imagination created images full of man's nightmarish acts of murder and betrayal.

Alee turned the page and screamed, "Look, the giant's eating a person!"

"Rosie! Move on, please," Vera stated.

"It's just a myth, Alee, that's *Saturn Devouring His Son,* one of Goya's Black Paintings covering the walls in his house. He was deaf by then, about 1820, but his idea of man's brutal cruelties had taken over his mind and he was possessed. Saturn was a Roman god who thought his offspring would overtake him, so he killed..."

"Stop, Rosie, that's enough about blood and death...Alee doesn't like Goya anyway, he's too realistic and reveals the ugliness in people most of the time."

"Okay, Vera, but he painted the truth in the most imaginative way ever," stated Rosie. "All I was saying was that the Prado was envied all over Europe for its Royal collection of Old Masters."

Rosie had followed the reports in the *Art News* magazine for years-how the Prado was notorious for its lax security and corrupt administrators. Curators were hired and fired left and right. The conservation and preservation departments were all but non-existent. Water-stained galleries threatened priceless Italian and Dutch art, from the Renaissance to the Baroque periods. It had been common knowledge for hundreds of years that many fakes and schools of artists were exhibited as the originals. For example, the Rembrandts were painted by his pupils, but signed by the master's name.

"You know, Vera, we should face the fact that the Captain was probably making copies of the Old Masters and selling them as long-lost originals," Rosie proclaimed, "and probably Tubby Dunbar set it up."

They both glanced over at Alee, who had been quiet too long. Her face looked like one of Picasso's puzzle portraits of Marie-Therese.

"Alee, you know in the past a lot of lying and cheating went on in the art world," Rosie began. "Sometimes unscrupulous dealers signed over a minor artist's signature with a more famous one, who painted in the same style...Like the Met's so-called Frans Hals was really a Judith Leyster, uncovered by x-rays. Many modern techniques in dating and testing wood or paint authenticity are used today."

Rarely did fakes pop up in the news, but they were out there anyway. Rosie was more than concerned—she shuddered at how close the Captain came to getting caught. It was really just a matter of following the paper trail. But his papers were stashed in a cigar box for over twenty years-and just found by his granddaughters. Obviously, the Captain was painting in the academic tradition of imitating or exactly copying museum masterpieces. These were the training techniques and methods used by all art students, as well as mixing and grinding paints in the master's studio. And of course, observing the tricks and skills of the trade for creating greatness. The finished copies of the artworks would be sold as being in the style or school of the artist. The signature and date were crucial in determining a copy. Both paintings are identical, nonetheless, and in the past a copy did stand in for the original, which was locked away in a vault somewhere. No one is the wiser, except for the owner and the experts, but it's easy to be fooled-so perfect is the copy. If the Captain signed the artists' signatures, it would have been deliberate and criminal, but without the signature, it's a legal, acceptable copy. If Tubby Dunbar had the last say in the matter, then the Captain never knew what hit him. Rosie, Vera, and Alee were getting warmer for sure.

Fakes, forgeries, and stolen art are really big business all over the world. Owning and living with a great piece of artwork is like being with a trusted, intimate old friend. Worth risking your life for, or even perhaps a life's sentence. Van Gogh held the record with the highest price ever—84 million dollars for *Irises* over ten years ago. Now it's a Picasso painting, worth nearly 104 million, and held in a bullet-proof vault at Fort Knox, no doubt.

It had to be that many copies were passed off as the masters' undocumented, studio version of the original-who's to say otherwise, when it was four hundred years ago. In the high-stakes art world there are substitutes, say at the Vegas Bellagio Museum-the real Rembrandt is in the safe, with a bona fide copy hanging in the gallery. "It's far too priceless to be hanging here in broad daylight, security alarm or not," was the manager's explanation. "Our visitors can't tell the difference anyway."

Usually the first question in an art discussion was, "Is that the original?" Of course it's always true for museums, and most often, if the truth be told, in private homes as well, since the super-rich are usually very proud of their personal collections. Many art magazines list the most famous collectors of Old Masters. Admiration is one thing, but rambling on about your priceless art collection does not give one prestige-but invites envy,jealousy and even thievery.

Loving art for its value is a far cry from what the Captain thought during his days and nights copying in the museums. His pursuit was a quest to find the root of their greatness and how these genius-masters changed our perception of reality throughout history. How they captured and froze a moment in time for all of us to admire.

They carried on traditions, told stories of life and death, giving us knowledge and understanding of what is most beautiful, tragic and true-in nature and mankind. All great art makes visible the invisible.

A trip to the Captain's old stand-bys, and a visit to the library, was the only way to discover the real truth-for Alee's sake.

It would be difficult to chip away at the so-called facts…how the Captain was imprisoned-trapped in a block of stone like Michelangelo's *Bound Slaves*-and only Tubby Dunbar could release him from his prison. Whatever hanging threads were left untied in the Captain's tapestry of masters, Rosie would have to connect them down in the Keys-where it all began and then unraveled. Weaving a hundred-knot-per-inch Oriental rug needed skilled fingers-same as a hammer and chisel for carving a statue. Rosie's weaving experience would surely come in handy, especially tracing the twists and turns of the *Topaz*'s meanderings in and about the islands. Organizing her approach to uncovering the true facts led Rosie to the library-a teacher's favorite hideaway and refuge. She had called and written to the public library first, making plans early, since the fall semester break was only a month way. It would be a long time before Alee would get her peace of mind about her great-grandpap. She never forgot about it, carrying around her art book and sitting up in the studio sorting postcards and photos—wondering how her great-grandpap painted so many pictures.

It was on the fall weekends, listening to Alee, that Rosie realized there was no turning back—they were on a mission to find out the truth. It wasn't a game or crossword puzzle—she needed to know how something good could have turned out so bad, and was still hoping he was just a victim. Late October up in the studio was like standing inside the walk-in cooler for an hour. The wind whistled and rattled the glass in the windows, while the dampness crept right into the bones. The master poster was still nailed to the wall, magic markers and crayons were scattered on the table. Rosie and Vera quietly cleaned up near the space heater in the corner-sadly piling papers into marked shoeboxes. Alee came barging in, yelling, "Nana's waiting for us downstairs...she told me to come and get you for dinner."

"Okay, Alee. Shut the heater off, Vera, this place is like a matchbox," Rosie said. "Don't tell Daddy either."

At suppertime, Pat and Phelia would sit at the front table watching the customers come and go. He would be raving about how fresh the bluefish tasted; "Just caught this morning, in the canyon." After the crowd died down, Lily, Alee, her sisters, and sometimes Cody and Jack joined them for steamers and fried clams. Then Rosie and Vera would muscle in on Phelia's baked stuffed lobster.

"Hey you two, get your own," she'd say.

"Oh, no you don't," the Baron would snap. "Order the bass or blue-fish, we'll be busy tonight, and there's not that many lobsters left."

"I'll just order the baked stuffed shrimp, it's better anyway, the lobster's only good for the claws," replied Rosie, "and let's order some vino rosso. Vera, give me the keys..."

"What?" the Baron shot back. "Get over to the cashier, Rosie...it's too early for that. Last night your face was as red as that lobster by eight o'clock."

"All right Dad, maybe about ten, when the kitchen closes," replied Rosie. "Before I go downstairs to the new bar to make some kamikazes, ha, ha."

Rosie and the Baron were always bantering back and forth about PR-ing for the club; her public relations being drinking and staying out till four in the morning. It was a long-standing father-daughter camaraderie, hinting at their mutual love and respect for one another. Rosie even asked, "Hey Dad, how about a couple of bucks to go to Woods Hole for my usual PR-ing..." and a four-inch wad of bills would come out of his pocket. Then he'd peel off five dollars, and chuckle, "Okay, here you go."

"Oh, and make sure that third floor is all locked up—we're closing next week and the windows have to be boarded up," the Baron instructed. "Hope you cleaned up the Captain's studio, it's like a fire trap up there."

"Okay Dad, Alee and Vera can help me tomorrow after brunch," said Rosie.

Everybody at the table stopped eating when Alee blurted out, "Wait...where are we putting Great-Grandpap's pirate map?"

In a split second, Vera said, "Oh, that old thing...we can hang it up at my house, okay Alee?"

The line was out the door by this time. Rosie jumped up to help the hostess take names. Just then the Baron yelled, "Never mind that, start clearing the tables and get the bus bucket...it's overflowing." Rosie was as fast as the dickens when it came to cleaning tables, and the Baron knew it. Dirty dishes would be gone in a minute and he'd start seating people himself. Everyone wanted to chit-chat with him, it was more than a thrill—it was one of the reasons why people came to the restaurant. First to be seen, and then to loosen up for the rock and rolling downstairs later. Going to the Baron's club was the highlight of the weekend for locals and weekend warriors—first going to Beach Heights by day for checking out the girls on the beach and then saying, "Meet me here later on tonight?"

Before the fire in 1912, the Cottage Club was the meeting place for prosperous summer families who lived in the Heights. The bluff had the most spectacular expanse of sea and sky. Like an enveloping Mark Rothko painting–a spiritual realm of quiet vibrations, and a deep, mysterious, color-field emptiness. At night the Blood-Buck-Thunder full moon would light up a pathway on the sea, from the shore all the way to Martha's Vineyard. It was a five-mile boat ride to the island and on a clear day you could see the reddish cliffs off Gay Head. Many lunch-timers sitting on the deck would wonder about the ferries going back and forth, asking "What's that?" It was the best spot for watching sunbathers and swimmers. Some hop-scotched over hot sand, while flip-floppers gingerly walked over pebbles and broken shells. The Baron often told the kitchen help to "Get down on the beach and rake up the dried piles of seaweed. Thank God we don't have a pier out there," he would say. "Can you imagine the insurance needed for boozing boaters to tie up at the dock? Not to mention the cost of fire and flood...which we don't have anyway."

The story goes that a fire started between the walls in the kitchen and wasn't discovered until early morning. It had been smoldering all night after the club had closed. Nobody got hurt, but the whole town came to mourn the grand dame's heap of ashes. Family lives were put on hold; no more morning coffee and newspaper, no more rainy day movies, pinball games, and "fish balls at three." Higher up on the bluff, the Terrace Gables crowd stayed through Happy Hour, drowning their loss of summer-by-the-sea with Cape Codders and steamers.

It took two years before a new Cottage Club was built by a Worcester businessman who'd summered on Green Pond for decades. The white clapboard building was sprawling-not a tall, looming monster blocking the neighbors' ocean view. The crowds flocked there as before, like hungry gulls circling the beach. The only other major disaster was the Hurricane of '44 when the pier was wiped out.

Pat Merrick had been in the Cape Cod vending business for about twenty years. He worked morning, noon, and night to make a go of it, and that included being on call. After the TV repair business, Pat discovered there was more money in cigarettes and pinball and pool tables—as long as they were in operation. There was a lot of driving to late night barrooms to keep him busy—a hectic schedule that groomed him for the restaurant business.

Rosie had just graduated from a small-town high school. She hated the town and thanked her lucky stars when they moved over the bridge. Her father happened to be in the right place at the right time, filling the cigarette machine at the Cottage Club, when the owner yelled, "Hey Pat, come over here when you're done, want to ask you something... I like you-the strong, silent type and not much of a drinker. You'd be good at this business."

"What are you talking about, Hank?" Pat asked. "Good at what?"

"How about leasing this place for a couple of summers...and if you want we can think about adding the option to buy as well."

Hank McCann was a regular kind of guy, getting on in years and hoping to find a hard-working, honest man to run his beloved Cottage Club. He figured Pat was just the guy to get the chance of a lifetime. And so it came to be—Pat Merrick and his family would have the best go-around anyone could ask for...a small dose of fame and fortune.

In the summer, Rosie returned to the city during the week to be with her husband. She fought the traffic at a slow crawl like everyone else on Sunday night. Her trunk was loaded up with red wine and seafood casserole. Sean Malone was ready and waiting for his sweetheart, and especially his favorite stuffed quahogs. The Baron never knew about Rosie's red cooler, for he sure would have had a thing or two to say about that. He never thought much of Sean. One time Rosie got a dozen red roses delivered at the bar—and her father said, "Who sent those...the dumb Mick?" Rosie never forgot that one, but she still made Sean ask her father for her hand in marriage the next year.

Sean Malone was not a yes-man, like the others working for the Baron. Not a liar or a thief either, more the silent, come-hither type with bedroom eyes. He and Rosie met working in the nightclub downstairs. And it wasn't love at first sight either-Rosie's cousin, Pat, brought him to work one summer; "Yeah, let's go to the Cape and get jobs at the Cottage Club. My uncle owns the place." Both guys were juice boys then, going for ice and glasses at the bartender's beck and call. Rosie was only twenty years old and sat at the cashier near the long bar—silent, unfriendly, and stuck-up. Little by little though, she noticed the tall hunk with curly reddish-brown hair-always surrounded by two or three girls at the end of the night. Not talking or hanging on them, but having a beer with the other workers. Still, every night girls followed him home for a party, and his roommates would gobble up the leftovers. Sometimes Sean would say, "Now go take care of my buddy over there."

It was more than a year or so before Rosie and Sean said more than hello and see you later...apparently he had all the patience in the world and was willing to wait for Rosie to come down off her high horse. One day, as if on cue, Rosie flirted first, with, "Hey, why don't you smile more?" And Sean was hooked for life.

It was two years before they went over the bridge together, and Rosie never looked back. It just so happened that she had gotten accepted into art school soon after they met and she was headed for the city anyway. Sean Malone was a city slicker and Irish to the core—pretty much a man's man, not a womanizer. Of course, the Baron thought of him as just another smartass galoot, giving free drinks away. Being alone and away from her family was traumatic, but Rosie had Sean and her weaving classes at MassArt to help sever the ties, and make her feel safe.

Sean's bar back stint for a couple of summers allowed him to fill in behind the bar a few times and from then on he was a bartender-with lots of cash in his pockets. It was a wild, irresponsible lifestyle—all the sex, drugs, cigarettes, and booze killed more than a few brain cells. Sean's best buddy the Bear would say, "What are ya doing hanging around with her...we gotta get going to MaryAnn's." But he still lived in the third-floor apartment with Rosie on Chiswick Road ... joking about his family, how the dirty Dolans dished it up with the Malones. He told stories of how his father gave the cousins land in Ireland after seeing them living in squalor. Land he inherited, but which sat idle for generations. Sean swore one day he'd become an Irish citizen—with all four grandparents born there.

Rosie and Sean experimented and partied along with a whole generation of free spirits. Quaaludes, a hit of sunshine or windowpane, and maui-wowie were plentiful. Rosie's later travels to Europe with an ex-boyfriend left Sean in limbo, and he was off to San Francisco. It took a long time to learn—but it felt like true love and nothing was going to stop her from proving it. When they first lived at the Grafton, the guest house across the street from the Club, the sexual tension was so thick you could cut it with a knife. Finally they went up to room nine and did it. Everyone else was smoking pot downstairs and swore they saw electric sparks and blinking lights. It was the first time of a thousand times thereafter. Ten years later they got married. The only request Rosie ever made was, "We can't get married until you get a job with benefits," and Sean had waited long enough. He started driving a bus for public transportation-a far cry from bartending.

Rosie and Sean never talked seriously about having children. And she had her share of abortions. No plan was ever set in place and it got too late—in their forties—to start a family. Sean had his regrets, and told himself he was too old now to be a father, and Rosie never made her mind up one way or the other. It just wasn't a priority, more like an afterthought, she told her sisters. Living without kids was either totally selfish or fate-no problems or tragic accidents to mess up your life. Then, of course, there's no grandchildren or legacy either. Rosie had no clue—was she a coward or courageous. The truth is as elusive and relative as God. The ideas occurred over and over in Rosie's mind and came out in her tapestries—faces, the sun, moon, and stars-especially the trees of life. As if her feelings grew from a bare tree into a flowering maple—colorful, strong, and sweet. A perfect description of her white knight-Sean Malone.

The fall semester started right after Labor Day. Rosie was teaching art history at a small New England college near Boston. Many students believed they had all the time in the world to be wasting. But twenty years later, bliss or not, looking back at fifty is an eye-opener. Like when the Mamas and Papas sing "Youth is wasted on the young," and "Those were the days my friend, we thought, they'd never end"…oh yeah, those were the days-and then you're in a mid-life crisis.

Thanksgiving recess snuck around the corner and students were scrambling to find out about final papers and exams. The Cottage Club had been shut tight since Halloween. It was fun working with Vera on Sundays, while the Baron was out fishing-but now it was just a memory. Rosie had been on the phone with Lily and Vera talking—"What pies and vegetables are you bringing to Mom's house? Oh, and when is the Disney trip scheduled…"—when Sean yelled in from the living room, "Hey, wait a minute, where do you think you're going?"

Rosie whispered, "Gotta go and give Sean the bad news." It wasn't the first time Rosie had gone to Disney with her sisters and the kids, but Sean felt left out this time around.

"Vera made all the reservations for January—and that's when school's out. Florida is so cheap in the winter when you book a Disney package ahead of time," Rosie explained.

"How long are ya going for?" he asked.

"Well, I need an extra two weeks to look up Papap's friends down in the Keys…guess I'll leave right after New Year's," Rosie said.

"That's great, you go on vacation and spend a thousand bucks, and I get to work overtime," Sean complained. "Go ahead, have fun with the kids…I'll be fine here with Spanky and Beansie. Who's in the Keys, anyway?"

Rosie shot back, "Well, Alee and Vera are trying to figure out what happened to the Captain's Old Master paintings, and want to see if his partner, Tubby Dunbar, is still alive. It could take a week."

Of course Rosie felt apprehensive about the reunion with the boss-man, and scared about what she might discover, but there was no need to worry Sean. Only Alee and Vera knew the details of his shaky Atlantic double-crosses. And if any crew members were still alive, they were long in the teeth and short of memory for sure. Rosie felt like the time she was sledding with Sean in the Arboretum—unable to stop and heading straight for a tree. But he steered out of it like a pro-just like she had to do for the Captain, try to figure out all three sides to the story; Papap's, Tubby Dunbar's, and the truth. No matter what she uncovered in Key West, chances are it was going to be ugly. But proving the Captain was trapped, heading for harm's way by Tiger was more important.

Towards the end of the Falling Leaves or Hunter's moon, Beach Heights became a veritable ghost town. Still, the Baron insisted on staying open on the weekends—to have his bluefish special nights. Alee knew better than to discuss our collage, and when she got carried away, Rosie quickly turned it around; "Alee, what's the painting you were talking about...the triptych of the Garden of Eden, Earthly...and Hell? Finish your steamers and we can look at the art book."

Quizzing Vera and Alee on the most famous paintings in the world was like solving the riddle of the sphinx-it depended on asking the right question. Once in a blue moon, though, they became so enraptured of a painting, they tranced-out to another time and place. The artist's imagination and symbolism is a powerful hypnotic and usually overwhelms the senses. The big color pull-out of Bosch's *The Garden of Earthly Delights* never failed to inspire fear, joy, and immense wonder—all at the same time. The most Freudian, surreal, and moralistic painting ever created, besides some of Salvador Dali's twentieth century erotic nightmares, was the

Prado's triptych; *The Garden of Earthly Delights,* with Paradise, Earth, and Hell panels connected together like an altarpiece, c. 1500. Alee usually ran to the desk drawer for a magnifying glass, to see all the evil creatures, fruits, and nudes close-up. The fantastic rock formations in the background look like they belong on Mars.

This complex and symbolic allegory was derived from medieval folktales, alchemy, and bestiaries. Hieronymus Bosch was probably a member of a religious brotherhood-a cult of alchemists who strived to turn base metals into gold. Many glass phials and mysterious combinations are depicted throughout the landscapes, from thistle flowers to test tubes; fishes, eggs, and strawberries to giant birds and unicorns. Rosie explained the iconography to Alee and Vera over and over, but they were too mesmerized and distracted to comprehend the details.

"Go from foreground to the middle and then back...start on the left side.

"If you're ready to listen, first look at Adam and Eve...even in Paradise, strange and sinister trees, reptiles, and three-headed birds symbolize their Fall from grace. A red-haired Christ, a cat and mouse, and peeping owl all indicate medieval ideas of good and bad," Rosie lectured. "The best way to see the bizarre happenings is to read the text interpretation while looking at the specific symbols. It's a kind of detailed realism-expressing how lustful sinners are doomed to hell. But the frolicking naked figures look like they're celebrating life; especially the bathers in the middle...only the parade of various animals with male riders suggest beastly appetites and sexual intentions. Some historians believe that Bosch is condemning sex—it's hard to say, with all the hugging and kissing...there's seven deadly sins, so..."

"Hey, is anyone really having sex?" Vera blurted out. "No, I mean..."

"Don't worry, Aunt Vera, I already know about it..." Alee smiled.

"Well, really, it's been analyzed to death and no one can say one hundred percent for sure-but probably not. Try to find the face of Bosch_wait," Rosie warned, "you gotta see what's going on in the Hell painting."

For Alee, the image of Hell was the most terrifying and shocking incrustation of devouring demons ever imagined. Fires of damnation in the background are ruled by a knife penetrating two ears. The cracked body of the eggman stands in the center—with Bosch staring right back at us, thinking God knows what. Most likely though, he, along with all people, priests and nuns included, are corrupt sinners. And the head ruler—the bird-king with an upside-down pot for a crown—sits on a high chair eating a damned soul, while black crows fly out his ass. The black putrid pool of water below receives his human excrement, while someone vomits on one side and another shits coins into it. No other artist comes close to this portrayal of torture and punishment. Damned souls are stabbed and strung up by musical instruments of pain-like the prison guard in the *Silence of the Lambs* torture cage.

Explaining human weakness to Alee was like sinking into quick sand—the more that was said, the more you tried to cover it up. Bosch's pessimistic view of humankind was not her world; but just a fantasy world—on another planet somewhere. Rosie reminded her, "Bosch is like a teacher giving us a visual lesson about how wicked, selfish, and sinful ways lead us into Hell...where we get punished for our bad deeds. Some might say it's justice for a morally infected society-bad karma here sends us to Hell." Alee would never know about sex, sins, and evil. She could see and understand the lessons to be learned in great art though-taking her to the highest levels of both tragedy and beauty.

Rosie continued to quiz Alee about what she saw during each time period, explaining how throughout history people had many different beliefs in God, nature, and family life. "Art challenges you to think about that, to read the messages through the symbolism and to see if the story is the same for us today-and if we've learned from the past." As soon as Alee's big moon eyes crinkled up, Rosie knew her attention span had been maxed out. Her years may have been short, but Alee possessed a lifetime of curiosity. She had a heightened sense of awareness of everybody around her and it spilled over when it came to art. The connections and associations she made were uncanny and remarkable for a young mind. Instead of exploring dance moves and boys, Alee wondered about still lifes, dragonflies, and portraits.

All of Lily's kids were suntanned and waterlogged that summer, except for Alee. She was far too serious about her great-papap's paintings. Rosie tried to keep it simple for Alee; "The dove is a fragile bird who flies...but when it holds an olive branch in its beak, it symbolizes peace... just like the details in the Captain's work. Look real close at the image, trust your eyes and ask yourself, does it seem sad, happy, serene, violent, beautiful, or ugly? Always ask why, Alee, why this or that color...and the painting will speak to you."

Vera usually watched Alee's face; giving her a reassuring hug after one of Rosie's lengthy explanations. "Don't worry, honey, people in Bosch's paintings are just playing...and yeah, some go to hell, but that's not you or us...you're more like Alice in Wonderland."

"No Vera, she's Dorothy in Oz, listening to 'Somewhere Over the Rainbow'-that's how fantastic you feel when finally you see the light."

"Hey, we gotta go and set up for dinner. C'mon on, Alee," Vera ordered.

It wasn't long before Alee was back in school, running track and figure-skating three times a week. It was a major relief that she had practice on the weekends and friends to hang out with—Vera and Rosie were making all kinds of incriminating ties between the Captain's museum jaunts and the *Topaz*'s excursions. It could have blown up in their faces while Alee was there sorting the postcards. In fact, Alee had stopped popping in the restaurant and would only call once a week to get her art history assignment from Rosie. She didn't even ask about the map anymore. It only came up when Vera talked about plans for the Disney trip.

"Oh yeah, Alee, we're all going on the African safari ride through the jungle, and of course, the Tower of Terror!"

"Hey Vera, tell Alee to look up Gauguin's *Day of The God*, one of his Tahitian paintings…she knows it's about the natives living in Paradise," Rosie yelled. "The colors and design look a lot like the Captain's island murals down in Woods Hole-with pirates and boats everywhere."

Alee was back on the phone a couple of hours later, asking, "Why are the naked girls lying around eating fruit with flowers in their hair? And the blue god just stands and protects them?"

"Well, yes, he's watching over his 'noble savages' in Paradise, guarding an uncorrupt, beautiful world from a false civilization. That's the bold, visible truth with Gauguin, Alee, he painted innocence."

Towards the end of the semester, with Christmas two weeks away, Rosie finished her last batch of grades for the registrar. She daydreamed about the Florida trip, while a Christmas Eve nor'easter blew in on the Long Cold Night full moon. They were snowed in for days. Delivering presents would have to wait for the gang down on the Cape. Rosie and Sean had a roaring fire, rum-spiced eggnog, and dancing to Frank Sinatra to keep them busy. Every time "New York, New York" came on, the Baron's goodnight theme song at the Club, tears streamed down Rosie's face.

Whenever Alee called up to get her art fix for the week, Lily interrupted the conversation; "Let me talk to Aunt Rosie…"

"Okay, just a sec…hey, it's almost time for Disney, did you write to Tubby Dunbar yet?" Alee whispered. And she was gone before Rosie could answer.

"Oh hi, what is it, Lily? I wanted to tell Alee where to find the hidden Mickeys…"

"It's about Vera, she's wound up like the Energizer bunny, planning every day down to the exact minute," complained Lily.

It was Vera's pet peeve that going to Disney with five adults and four kids needed a set plan of attack—in order not to miss the best rides, exhibits, and parades. She even had the fast-passes reserved for the rides at night. Vera always had an itinerary established for her Disney trips, with dinner reservations at the best places. And as a member and stockholder, she got all the perks, too. Each one of us got a color-coded daily calendar of events and admission times for all the rides. Lily thought this sounded more like boot camp than a Disney vacation. But it all melted in your mouth like butter. We all still checked with Vera to make sure everyone could meet together for character sightings and Rock & Roller flights.

It was going to be a super-packed ten-day visit, confirmed and reserved months ahead of time. Her husband Teddy kept quiet, never doubting that the family vacation would be one for the books.

Teddy and Vera had been married only five years when he found out about her compulsive disorders. When they bought a new house, Vera made him strip off his landscaping work clothes and mud-caked boots before coming into the house. Freezing, standing naked in the garage, he'd bolt in the door and hug her until he got warmed up. The only time he was upset was when Vera turned his music off so she could watch another movie. Her dust-free, everything-in-its-place perfection was just another kind of addiction running through most everybody in the Merrick clan—from coffee and cigarettes to booze and gambling. Not to even mention every family's nightmare-drugs. But Vera's nagging and fussing didn't last long. Hard-working Teddy worked off his own fears from six am to six pm, and was too tired to argue. He just got a tape recorder and made Vera listen to herself. "That's not me...bitching in a munchkin voice non-stop," she cried. Teddy just grinned and that was the end of that. Vera never nagged again, not with her six tiny pups running helter-skelter within a year. "Dog-lady of Parsons Land" became her new nickname from then on out.

For Vera and all the kids the Florida vacation was like shooting the rapids one day and sprinkling fairy dust over all the hidden Mickeys the next. Tinkerbell was running through Alee's blood. It turned out to be the best hand-holding Disney trip of all—we all walked around with star-topped wands, waving them over the rides. There were boat rides, fireworks, a red-white-blue blinking musical light show off the balcony of the Wilderness Lodge. And Vera sat like queen for a day over the hoedown dinner theater As cowboys sang and danced, Cody fell head-first into his fried chicken and strawberry shortcake, he was so tuckered out—and we all laughed till we cried. The Disney vacation was one of Alee's happiest times...she even got chosen from the crowd that night and twirled the lasso on stage, shouting, "He-haw partner!" It was the Disney trip of a lifetime-with memories of Alee.

Her one and only stage performance-and it all ended far too soon. She wanted to go again on her Make-A-Wish trip. The last time Vera and Teddy went again it was for the cancer Run for Your Life marathon—in memory of Amber Bailey. Teddy ran with "Amber B -— 1990-2003" emblazoned on his T-shirt. None of us ever felt the same about Mickey and Minnie again–we were always missing Alee, just sitting and staring up at the clouds. Crowds of people would parade by, but the road to the castle was empty. From time to time, her ghost would walk by... but it was just another pretty, pony-tailed twelve-year-old, falling behind her family.

During the last few days, in between the Haunted House and the Rockin' Roller Coaster, Alee stayed in the back of the pack listening to Rosie and Vera battle about what to do in Crab Key.

"Look at the map again, Vera," Rosie demanded, as she pulled it out of her purse. "The mother and daughter went down near Key...go get lemonade ices, Alee."

"Wait, they were killed where?" Alee shouted.

"No, no honey...we don't know that," Vera interrupted. "Here's money for the drinks."

"Every time she sees the map, Rosie, Alee goes whoopie...watch what you say...just go check with the police first...see if anybody was arrested."

"Oh, great, Vera, that's really drawing attention to the Captain," replied Rosie. "What if they re-opened the case and disappearances.... no way."

There was time in the morning for a swim and some Disney toys. While the others got packing, Rosie ordered another piña colada and checked over her Key West reservations and directions. She had seven days to look up Tubby Dunbar and locate the Captain's old haunts. *Better start in the library,* Rosie thought, *see the microfiche for old newspapers...Wonder if the* Topaz *is shipwrecked somewhere? And maybe his paintings are still hanging up in a couple of the local gin mills.*

Vera hugged Rosie good-bye, whispering, "Find out for Alee. Think he could have a new crew of pirates now?"

"Naw, he's too old," Rosie replied.

Alee came barreling over, throwing her towel down-ready to jump in the pool. "Mom's packing but Dad and Cody are going down the dragon slide one more time," she squealed. "Aunt Rosie, when are you leaving? Will you call me at home?"

"Of course, look for a postcard or two...gotta go early in the morning, honey," Rosie smiled. "Probably go to the library first and then look for Valentine's boarding house. The Captain practically lived there sketching the locals...guess it was like the Foles-Bergere in Paris—dancing and singing at night," Rosie explained. "Like the Moulin Rouge paintings by Toulouse-Lautrec—look them up Alee, very expressionistic with loud, sad-looking women dancing the high step."

"Just like Great-Grandpap's pictures at the restaurant?" Alee said.

"Yeah, especially check out the people in Degas's *The Absinthe Drinker*—two lost souls staring off in a smoky cafe. They're full-page color reproductions in the art book," Rosie replied.

Vera plunked her duffle bag down and hugged Rosie. "Never mind the art lesson...we gotta go, Alee, take care, sis. What's the number for the B & B?" she asked. "Well, just call right away, all right?"

Lily came rushing out to the pool, rounding everybody up. She kissed Rosie good-bye, whispering, "Love you dearly, sis, please be careful." Vera turned to wave good-bye, her arm around Alee, and Rosie felt three hearts beat as one.

Part IV

The Old She-Wolf Full Moon

As Rosie drove over the miles-long bridge past Key Largo, she was awestruck—deep open space engulfed her. The Big Bang in reverse. She was floating inside an aquamarine gemstone; luminosity wrapped her up in a blanket of shimmering white highlights. *Abstract and sensual like a Rothko,* thought Rosie, a vast, throbbing color field inspired by nature, then transformed into symbolic waves of emotions. A true painter of the sublime and subtle mysteries of nature. Like the transcendentalists-he was one with Thoreau and his *Life in the Woods.* Only Rothko's *Blue and Green* expresses the beautiful and the tragic all at the same time. Thoreau's and Rothko's two sides of human nature could be the classic *ut pictura poesis*-how literature and fine art feed off one another.

Anxious and overwhelmed, Rosie finally arrived at the southernmost tip of Florida. She took a left off Main to Coral Key. Soon a rambling, weather-worn mansion brought her to a dead stop. Seagulls perched atop the widow's watch and a row of rainbow-colored rockers lined the wrap-around porch. The bric-a-brac sign over the entrance spelled out "Conch

Haven" in scallop shells. The B & B looked deserted, and only a wandering pair of poodles greeted her. For a century, the big Victorian had sat right on the beach, surviving hurricanes and hundred-degree summer heat. A lighthouse on the jetty housed a blinking warning light. Rosie felt disoriented and gazed out to the horizon—the only way to right her mind and body. But it was Alee's voice that shook her up now, as she remembered when she said, "What happened, did they all drown?"

Only Tubby Dunbar knows that, and he could be dead in the head by now, Rosie thought. Quickly grabbing her bags, she palmed the tin bell at the front desk. A bandana-wrapped servant girl called out, "Miss, over here…we can go upstairs to your room first." She unlocked room 9 and waved good-bye. Rosie dropped her bags and whipped back the bedspread to check out the sheets. They were sandy but clean.

She needed to wake up and decided to go for a swim. Several Impressionist seascapes hung on the walls, signed by an Abigail Riley. Walking through the front parlor, she snatched up a bunch of postcards picturing the Victorian facade and Conch Haven's address. "Wonder where the desk clerk is…better peek at the local newspaper before going into town too," Rosie said out loud. A straw-hatted lady carrying a plastic bag of seashells said, "Are you our new guest, miss?"

"Yes, hello…just got here, thought everyone was on siesta or something," Rosie replied.

"Pretty much, see you later," and she was off.

The crystal clear sea was like bath water—warm and relaxing. Rosie dripped dry and scribbled a quick message to Vera and Lily; "Paperwork and map all in order. Went for a dip already, but it's time to walk into town…keep your fingers crossed, later, Rosie." She slipped the sun dress over her suit and eased into her sandals. Beach plum bushes and wild pink roses lined the path into town. Right after the post office, she spied another flag waving up ahead. *Looks a lot like P-Town around here,* Rosie thought. *Great, there's the public library…perfect timing.* She settled down with the antiquated microfiche recorder, when a frizzed-top lady wearing granny glasses tapped her on the shoulder and asked, "How far back ya going, dearie?"

"Hi, don't know, maybe 1920 or so." Rosie hesitated. "Who are you?"

"Hazel MacIssac, been here forever," she replied.

"Did the *Key West Banner* always have a police blotter?" Rosie inquired. "Thought maybe they'd list arrests or investigations."

"Yeah, here's all the court procedures...which one ya lookin' for?"

Rosie turned and looked hard into her cataract eyes, then back at the screen. The bold words read: "The *Topaz* and crew charged with the disappearance of stolen property, kidnapping, and extortion..."..

"Are these headlines for real?"

"You mean about Tubby Dunbar's trial?" Hazel asked.

"You remember it all right?" Rosie asked.

"Well, of course, biggest brouhaha this town had ever seen," Hazel snapped.

She rolled the microfiche to the 1926 *Banner* with the front-page headlines spelling, "TOPAZ INC. INDICTED." The entire crew had been rounded up. The black-and-white photo had five men in handcuffs, heads bowed down. The names read: Tiberius Dunbar, Bullard Merrick, Malcolm Lawrence, Roscoe Beauregard, and Jim "Porky" Riley.

It took more than an hour to read all the news clippings for the next eight months—scandalous accusations fed the imaginations of locals and visiting journalists. All the charges—from kidnapping to forgery—amounted to serious jail time. Rosie sat dumbfounded, suspended in time, until Hazel tapped her lightly on the arm. "Come in the back for a cup of tea, honey," she whispered.

"Okay, getting to the dismissals anyway," Rosie replied. "Just wanted to see what happened to Captain Merri."

Hazel was not some old, senile biddy; she had been teaching the three R's for more than thirty years. Rosie followed her into the tiny den behind the circulation desk.

"So, you knew the Captain?" Hazel asked.

"Oh yeah, he was my grandfather," Rosie replied.

"Well, he was the poet-laureate around here...no, the painter-in-residence is better. In demand and very popular...painting the riff-raff, mucky-mucks, and tourists strolling the pier. Too bad about what happened; his own skipper turned him in," Hazel explained. "The raid on his studio above Valentine's was a total set-up. All the boat schedules, photos, and customer receipts were stamped TOPAZ, INC.-but his boss was the ringleader. His little girl, Josie, hung on to him all the way to the police station."

"What? Whose little girl?" Rosie exclaimed.

"Valentine's and the Captain's-she was almost eight years old then," Hazel said matter-of-factly to a drop-jawed Rosie.

Rosie felt like she was caught in a riptide, the repercussions of her digging became the waves quickly spreading further out, breaking up the peaceful past. Visions of drowning and masked men ransacked her brain. *Better to be attacked by mosquitoes and snapping turtles than to find out the Captain was all lies and deceit,* Rosie thought. He couldn't have known about drownings!

A major art scam and forgery business had been exposed. The charter tours and sport fishing expeditions were intertwined with such precision that the *Topaz* operated below the radar screen for years. The head honcho, Tubby Dunbar, was a mastermind at juggling and coordinating the schedules—abroad and in the bay. A multi-faceted prism yielding a fortune in priceless fakes of Old Masters. And like a puppet, the Captain played his role for the boss—doing what he loved more than his own family; painting with the eyes of his master-heroes. Copying in the most famous museums in the world was not his crime—but a once-in-a-lifetime chance to experience his greatest love.

The evil criminal in the whole scheme was the one who got away—T.D. was like an alligator hiding in the swamps. The king of predators, feasting on greed and murder. The level of betrayal was devastating all around, especially for the Captain, who played the patrons for his share of the profits. The charges and evidence were never conclusive. A convoluted paper trail and some faded sketchbooks were the only clues left for the F.B.I. to unravel. The years went by and the leads got cold over the Atlantic. And in Rosie's mind, she was thankful for their unfinished business and lack of dead bodies.

Hazel's voice jolted her back to reality. "There's a lot of his paintings hanging up at Valentine's, have you seen them?"

"Oh, no, better beat feet over there now...is she still around?" Rosie asked.

"Most all the time, take Seapit Road at the end of the street," Hazel said. "It's a cabaret now...one of the best shows in town."

Rosie shook Hazel's hand softly and said, "Thanks for being so nice to me...hope to see you again. Oh, how do I find out about the obituaries from that time?"

"Come back and we'll look them up tomorrow," she said softly.

They walked out together and Rosie turned to wave good-bye. She had to move aside quickly, making room for the janitor sweeping off the entrance stairs. Taken aback by his Rip van Winkle appearance, she asked, "Excuse me, sir, have you worked here long?"

When the grizzled, wrinkled, worn face looked up, Rosie fell back against the railing. He was a Captain look-a-like with white hair, bushy eyebrows, and sad, droopy eyes. His face was like an over-tanned baseball glove. Around his neck was a sailor's rope necklace with a shark's tooth and a branch of pink coral dangling from a center-squared knot, just like the Captain's.

Rosie had seen this man in a small black-and-white photo up in the studio. There was a shoebox full of old snapshots, but his was stamped *TOPAZ*. "You're the man sitting with my grandfather in front of Billy's Bait & Plukit-Bucket Shop," exclaimed Rosie.

"Who's your grandpa?" he asked.

"The artist, Bull Merrick, well, Captain Merri down here," replied Rosie.

His head picked up quickly and the wise look in his eyes made Rosie touch his shoulder firmly. "Think we could sit down for a minute and talk?" They walked outside and sat down in the shade, and all the while Rosie silently held his hand. The old gent began to mumble something about working in a fish shack on the bay for the *Topaz* boss, Tiger Dunbar. "Yeah, he was big and mean, always hustling the customers onto the boat. Taking their pictures with a little Kodak, yelling to me, 'Hey Billy, hurry up with the chum and coolers.' "

"What's your name?" Rosie asked.

"Billy Jason...came down here from New Orleans back in '25. Just started fishing and shrimping over in Conch Bay, and met the boys. My cousin, Rocky Breauregard, was already netting and harpooning off the *Topaz*, and there was a lot of fish to haul in and gut.

"Lost these two fingers in the ropes. After that the boss put me in the bait shop—and called it Billy's...hey, how'd ya find me?"

"Well, you're a bonus...the plan was to find Tubby Dunbar," Rosie confessed.

"You mean Tiger? Heard he lives in Key Marco. Can't recognize him anymore; hunchbacked and half-mad."

"Saw him awhile back at my Grandpap's funeral...he looked bad then," replied Rosie. "He mumbled something about the Captain's studio and if there were sketches around, then he walked away and that was it."

Rosie kept an eye on Billy and realized he was not just another rum-runner, flim-flam fisherman from the Bahamas. She hesitated and explained, "After me and my sister found some postcards and photos stashed in the floorboards of the studio, we knew something wasn't right. Came down here to find out and talk to Tubby Dunbar. It's pretty crazy, but we loved Papap and needed to know what happened."

Rosie was trying to stay as calm as possible, but running into Billy was not a coincidence, more like fate. *Best to let him talk,* she thought. *T.D. did him in too-wonder why he's not sleeping with the sharks.*

"Well, miss, you have a generous spirit in your eye like Bull. We were mates, trapped like rats and didn't know about no cover-up."

Rosie held her breath. "What cover-up?"

"When the boss took the Missus and her daughter out—the fire below made them jump overboard, and the hammerheads did the rest, most likely. Never found the bodies. He got the Captain and the Mister to go to Spain for some painting work," Billy said, his head turned away.

"Wait, the paper said they drowned while the Mister was away," Rosie stuttered.

"Jumping boys, gotta get back to work, miss, else they'll can me. You take care, be wary of Tiger, he's a Jekyll and Hyde. Go straight to the end here, near Key Marco take Sandy Neck. Probably knotting his nets... bring him some fruit and nuts, cracking walnuts makes him ramble, and he forgets to lie," explained Billy.

He waved slowly and yelled, "See ya later."

Rosie stood up and shouted, "Hey, Billy, where's Valentine's?"

"Behind the post office, towards the beach. Take care now."

She stood watching him shuffle back into the library - the Captain's buddy was still living proof of the *Topaz* crew. Rosie's mind was twisting and turning like the teetering coffee pots in Max Ernst's *Elephant of Celebes*. They stand next to the red-gloved headless mannequin, which points up towards the pot-bellied monster—looking like a Tubby Dunbar in disguise. It was a repulsive, menacing creature, with tusks for a tail and machine parts for his long snout. Everything is backwards and upside down, even fish and keyholes float in the sky. The nightmarish world of Surrealism was fragmented and ambiguous, full of bizarre juxtapositions-like the hidden agendas in people's lives. Rosie was seeing the Captain in a new light and it was flickering fast. She could not explain to Alee and Vera how the Captain was manipulated like everyone else. Might as well tell them how the cow jumped over the moon or how Rene Magritte's *Eyeball in the Sky* was a reflection symbol of our own changing and destructive world-a world we choose to live in or seek to escape from.

The neon sign had blinking outlined letters in yellow and red-VALENTINE'S. On auto-pilot, Rosie walked slowly towards the colors and pushed open the glass entrance door. She found herself staring at big, bold, 1940s movie posters in the hallway. The violent, explicit, sexual imagery struck a note of fear inside Rosie for the first time-fear that Tubby Dunbar's mean streak ruined and ended dozens of innocent lives.

The tix-box window read "Dinner-Theatre/Cabaret Tonight." She picked up the playbill off the ledge and read, "a hoot & screaming good time for all—come and play with the kings and queens." On the back was a short "History of Valentine's Victorian Dance Hall."

The cookie-cutter, mansard-roofed mansion was built back in 1889 by Colonel Grenadier Valentine—in the decorative Queen Anne stick and shingle style. Brightly painted spirals on the outside screamed at the teak and cedar detailed moldings on the inside. A turreted corner tower room loomed upward, topped by a swinging mermaid weathervane. Tourists knew it as the "gingerbread house," but the local historical society deemed it a landmark on their summer gardens-by-the-sea tour.

Twenty-five years later clapboards were hanging with peeling paint curls all over the facade. "The Mermaid House" was a sailor's delight—more like a brothel than a hotel. Runaways and illegals worked in the kitchen and laundry rooms. Valentine Grenadier, the mistress-madam, was the great-great-granddaughter of the Colonel. Rosie found out from the microfiche that Topaz Inc.-aka T. Dunbar—had been a silent partner, who ran it into bankruptcy a decade later.

"Imagine Hopper's House by the railroad and the *Psycho* mansion," Rosie explained to Vera and Alee later, "full of damaged, lonely souls, numbing their pain with opium, sex, booze, and music. You can still smell the damask rose potpourri...now it's like a Moulin Rouge with vulgar impersonations by drag queens. Got a ticket for tomorrow night, Vera, and tell Alee I love her....call ya later."

Rosie walked the mile or so along the beach road, kicking up broken shells and watching the clammers out on the mudflats. Sleek, noisy cigarette boats skidded off the water in the distance, as if in mid-flight. Some dodged the off-shore windmills or scooted on past the charter boats. Just coming into view from behind a massive sand dune was a sprawling, Palm Beach-style stucco villa. Rosie stopped and looked around. "This has got to be private property," she said out loud. "Oh yeah, there's the No Trespassing sign…gotta get closer."

The faded and chipped concrete mansion looked like a huge pink conch shell. It was surrounded by a chain-link fence overgrown with stringy vines. The driveway had been padlocked, with a rusty Keep Out sign chained to the gate. Rosie stood still and listened-the waves hitting the shore blocked out all but the distant yelping of a dog. Walking around the beach side, through sea grass and briars, she gasped at the guano-stained stucco and thought of the seagull turds covering the jetty at Beach Heights. Even Dali's ants feasting on watches in *The Persistence of Memory* comes to mind-how the passing of time turns us old and rotten. How Nature eventually reclaims her territory by destroying and creating.

Rosie's heart was pounding along with the tide rolling in, and she wanted to leave this godforsaken place behind. A black spiral staircase climbed up the back side; hanging bougainvillea, wild roses, and hibiscus were in full bloom strangling the black iron trellis. Old garden tools leaned up against the wall. *Someone tends this garden,* Rosie thought, *making something beautiful out of nothing.* Like painting, the creative act is like a miracle, or a brilliant flash lighting up the imagination. Flowers, art, music—nature's gift of sublime beauty brought forth by human hands. Then, in an instant, a hurricane blows it all out to sea.

Just the lesson Rosie got in art school; skill and drawing techniques can be taught, but imagination cannot—that's when sparks fly. And that's when all kinds of gardens bloom, getting overgrown in the hot sun.

Rosie sat on top of a crumbling stone wall brushing off cracked moon shells, dropped long ago by gulls who had pecked out the innards. She followed the wall to the driftwood steps and looked down the stairs. Dragging rope strands behind him, a crooked figure climbed up slowly, leaning on a driftwood branch for support. Sniffing at his heels was a bony Irish wolfhound. Rosie jumped back, looking for a place to hide. *Just say you're lost, and don't get too close,* she thought.

The face of Tiger Dunbar stared hard at her and within seconds he growled, "Watch it." Fixing to grab a leg or arm, the mangy mutt then got whacked on the head by Tiger, who yelled, "Don't move, girl, this is private property and no one's invited here."

Shaky and stuttering, Rosie heard words come out of her mouth; "All right, sir, don't mean any harm...just looking for a family friend."

"What's in the bag?" he demanded.

"Some fruit and nuts...for a Mr. Tubby Dunbar," Rosie replied.

"Well, give 'em here then."

Rosie reached out and the hound snapped within an inch of her hand-white drool hanging from its jaw.

"Down, Royal," he yelled, kicking him out of the way but missing by a mile-as if the dog knew what to expect. "What do you want with him anyway?" His wild eyes were fixed and glaring.

"He worked with my grandfather on the *Topaz*...is he still alive?" she inquired.

"Ah ha, that depends, girlie, course they tried...to get me," he shot back, with hardly a tooth left in his mouth. "The *Topaz* was all mine, yep, boss Tiger's sports cruiser. Who the hell was your grandpa?" Turning away with a wave of his hand, he headed on towards the house.

Alee and Vera won't believe this one, Rosie thought, as she followed him down a path lined with spiky pink roses and walnut shells. Off the veranda a salt-smeared French door was wide open. Out came a short, bespectacled man in a drab yamata saying, "Stop, you go now."

"What?" Rosie called out, "Mr...hey, excuse me, sir, can we talk for a minute?"

He said nothing, only a deep, throaty snoring sound stopped Rosie in her tracks—the old man and the hound had nodded off quicker than a snakebite.

Rosie stepped back, knocking into the Japanese gardener. He was silent now, shaking his head as he shuffled out the door. The room looked medieval; dusty draperies hung down to the floor and a sand-covered Oriental rug lay in front of a huge stone fireplace. Blocky, primitive animal sculptures took the place of furniture-like chacmool guardians-but covered by knotted fish nets, turning them into prisoners. *What a control freak,* mused Rosie, *or maybe he's getting ready to drown them, too.* Newspaper headlines flashed through her mind and Alee's face appeared; stubborn and waiting for the truth. As compassionate and profound as Rembrandt's *Return of the Prodigal Son*, she was full of love and family loyalty-far beyond her young years. But Alee was still vulnerable, just like the son who risked losing it all despite the old patriarch's warning.

Rembrandt would have recognized her sensitivity and kindness. They were an odd pair of soul mates—the Old Master and the young muse, with more than their share of sadness and tragedy. He painted over sixty self-portraits; each one a map of *his* heart and mind.

As Rosie's eyes shifted from T.D. to the animals, she thought of the Captain and his portrait paintings, signed "Coral Key"...Tiger, Lil Josie, Billy, Cleo, Rocky, and Valentine... *Could they be here hanging up here?* Just looking at the drapes covering the walls and the grand staircase was enough for Rosie to wonder... *Looks like the perfect hiding place.*

The hound started rubbing his matted fur into the carpet, then he rolled over on his back. She saw a belly scar from his butt up to his chest. *What an ugly bastard; looks mean, rotten, and nasty to the core like his master,* Rosie thought, *marred by the boss like everyone else...guess we're all afraid of Tubby Dunbar.*

He was asleep for only minutes, before Rosie peered into his black eyes, ready for strike mode. "So, what are you doing here, girl?"

"Captain Merri was my grandfather," Rosie replied. "Bull Merrick."

"That was a long time ago, over forty years since he's been here," T.D. stated matter-of-factly. "Yeah, we worked on the *Topaz* and ran a pretty good business together, too."

"Well, the Captain had a lot of stuff in his studio at my father's restaurant," said Rosie. "Mostly photos, postcards, and sketch books. It looks like he traveled a lot, visiting all the famous museums."

"Hey, I saw you up there, at Bull's funeral, right?" he blurted.

"Yeah, but never thought you'd remember that...my name is Rosie."

"That was a sorry day, all right, the Captain was my best friend...and it's a damn shame what everybody said about him," T.D. admitted.

"You mean none of it's true?" asked Rosie. The Captain couldn't remember.

"Well, we never killed anybody...made a lot of enemies though," he said. "The drownings were accidental, and we weren't even there! Bull and the Mister had gone to Spain to see the Goyas and I was at Billy's."

Rosie let him spit it all out, as he went into a tirade about how they persecuted and attacked him and the crew, but his body language said it all. Rosie thought of a weasel caught in a trap, ready to chew its leg off to get free. T.D. stood up, pacing and agitated, then went over to the window and leaned his head against the glass. He looked pathetic, hunched over like Quasimodo-lost and alone, about to jump. Rosie got a whiff of rotten fish from the opened French doors. *Better go before he snaps out of it,* she mused, *the calm before the storm...* Rosie kept seeing those black headlines and was terrified. She knew Tubby Dunbar was an unscrupulous adventurer, volatile and ruthless-the quintessential modern-day Bly. Only the *Topaz* crew couldn't mutiny—they already had bloody hands. He set them all up and left them holding the bag-the pawns in his chess game.

The walk back to the B & B was as hot and anxious as a Turner seascape—brilliant, glorious colors filled the sky. The setting sun blazed down behind the horizon, as in *The Slave Ship,* a tragedy at sea in 1824, made visible by the great English Romantic Joseph Mallord William Turner. Stormy gray skies are on the left where the shipwreck goes down, and sunlit clouds on the right side symbolize hope. It's a story about slaves thrown overboard by a corrupt captain to collect insurance—humankind at its worst, greedy and ready to collect on the weak and dying. Like the *Topaz,* soon to be sinking too...taking down Dunbar's victims. No doubt the Captain was blindsided, way across the Atlantic. *Maybe Turner had the right idea—tying himself to the mast of a ship to experience the elements and disasters caused by Nature's wrath,* Rosie thought. If the Captain had been with the crew on board, nothing would have happened. All he ever wanted was to be free to be an artist.

It was near suppertime when Rosie jumped out of the shower. As she wrote a couple of postcards, the red phone light started blinking. *Hope it's Vera, oh no, gotta get to the show,* Rosie thought. She slipped on a halter dress, grabbed a sweater, and was out the door. The dinner theater had already started when Rosie squeezed into a corner bar stool. She was glad it was next to the waitress area-the best way to get the scuttlebutt about the customers and staff.

"Rum twister, slippery nipple, sex-on-the-beach, and a sunrise," Chrissy, the redhead, yelled. "Keep your pants on, Gina, be there in a sec," the bartender hollered back. Up on stage the he-shes paraded and lip-synched to a player piano. All the tables were full of couples and locals, wide-eyed and half-drunk. Everybody was singing along to Gypsy Rose Lee's lyrics, "Let me entertain you...let me make you smile, and if you're real good, I'll make you feel good, we'll have a real good time oh yeah, we'll have a real good time."

The queens were kicking up their heels and throwing panties into the audience—a can-can affair, risqué, hilarious, and mesmerizing. Coming straight towards Rosie was a statuesque, cleavage-packed, red-lipped, bleached-blond amazon, well over fifty. It was Ms. Cleo, the boss lady, dressed for the kill.

"Chrissy, get me a raspberry-lime rickey, oh, no wait, a Tom Collins, iced," she demanded huskily. "Thanks, sugar."

By intermission, Rosie had scoped out Cleo's side table and after another Long Island ice tea, she sauntered over. "Excuse me, ma'am, could I speak to you about some old friends?"

"Well dearie, that depends on if I know them or not...don't talk much about the past, that's asking for trouble," she warned Rosie.

"It's about my grandfather, Captain Merri, he worked with Tubby Dunbar on the *Topaz*," she explained.

Cleo's face tensed up and her wrinkles showed underneath the Bondo. "That's a touchy subject around here...skeletons in the closet, my dear, can shake and rattle up the devil himself. My aunt Jo Valentine told me they found them in the cellar of the old Mermaid," Cleo rambled. "See those two portraits behind the bar...the Captain gave them to my aunt–that's me and Jo."

Rosie heard the piano gal tune up and then the lights dimmed. The mirrored disco ball started spinning right along with her brain. "Then you were friends with my Papap?" Rosie asked loudly.

"A lot more than that, dearie...oh, the second act is on, gotta get backstage...talk to ya later," Cleo declared.

"Wait a sec, is that Mr. Dunbar's pink house on Coral Key?" asked Rosie.

"Hell no, it's Augie Amelia's from the Carolinas, must be ninety now, or he's probably dead. Ask the nutcase, Tiger...he knows," Cleo replied. "Come over tomorrow about noontime...I'll be in the cabana out back."

The love-hate relationship between Tiger and Madam Josephine was mostly a business affair-between a lug and a lady. The Captain had her pastel portrait next to his self-portrait in the studio. He had painted her wearing a paisley turban, with her hands holding a deck of cards. Rosie always asked him who Madam Jo was, but he only mumbled, "Oh, that was a long time ago, sweets, she was a landlady who told everybody's fortune. We all loved her dearly."

Rosie figured out that the old Mermaid Inn had been a whorehouse for sailors and locals. The *Topaz* crew were regulars, stuffing the girls' bras with twenty-dollar bills every weekend. The Captain, like Toulouse-Lautrec, kept a sketchbook of all the lovelies and parlor games to amuse himself and remember the good times. Not like the Moulin Rouge dancing couples; more like a quick, colored sketch of his friends foolin' around-smoking and drinking.

Toulouse-Lautrec's paintings of life were more depressing. Madam Jo's café had been a fly-by-night bordello with "Josephine's Tarot & Palm Readings" in the back room. The Captain's portrait of her was bold and symbolic-she held a mother-of-pearl cigarette holder in her fingers and the *Book of Changes* was nestled against her chest. In the background the sun set on one side and the moon rose on the other, as if she were the hot sun by day and a full moon, cool and silvery, by night.

For Josephine, the yin and yang determined her predictions for the paying customers. Her face had black outlines, her jade green eyes dared you to say hello. *No wonder Papap kept this portrait*, thought Rosie. *Who could ever let such a provocative sexual creature like this out of sight.* It was the same as when Leonardo kept *Mona Lisa* with him always-until it was found in his palace studio after his death.

Portraiture is art history's form of revealing the artist's self or beliefs—reaching the highest levels of truth, power, and romanticism. All the details and colors symbolize the personality, establishing the sitter's status- like a memorial for posterity.

The self-portraits of the artists were an endless fascination for Rosie, who swore she could see all their loves, regrets, and painful secrets right on their faces. The self was one of those universal themes, along with God, Nature, and Death. Just as Leonardo said, "Watch strangers walking in the street...study their faces to see how their eyes become the windows of their souls." All types of emotional states of mind can be detected in his sketches. Leonardo's notebooks, famous for their mirror-writing, depict science, nature, and people-including the Vitruvian Man, clouds, water spirals, and a fetus in the womb. He even dissected corpses!

Hunting down the Captain's collection, thought Rosie, *is near impossible. Surely they've scattered in the winds by now.* The best part about his portraits was their harsh dose of reality and exaggerated facial features. His spontaneous, quick brushstrokes were like those of Frans Hals, whose *Jolly Toppers* revealed their love of life or *joie de vivre.* He also combined the expressionistic edge of Alice Neel's sitters, who twist and gesture uncomfortably. The Captain could easily uncover the sitters' inner voices, flaws, and failures. But usually the Captain masked and hid their miserable lives through the grinning faces-seriously overindulging, as if excess, not moderation, keeps their demise at bay, whereas Rembrandt's fears and disappointments are etched on his face for all the world to see-a profoundly moving depiction of loss and age.

The pastel caricatures by Captain Merri never flattered or airbrushed the wrinkles, moles, and scars of the sitters, like Gainsborough, Reynolds, or Sargent's grand-manner portrait style. No, the Captain's portrayals were just as brutal and honest as a Van Gogh-full of raw energy and emotion.

Rosie's thoughts clicked and jumped around like a finger on a TV remote. She had planned out the morning and afternoon ten times already. *Got to get to Cleo first, maybe if she knew about Alee, his great-granddaughter, she'd want to finally set the record straight...*

Rosie woke up in a panic. The phone was ringing off the hook. She realized that days had passed without a word to anyone back home. "Call me back, Rose, where have you been?" was the phone message her husband left.

She dialed him up in a panic. "Sorry, honey, been trying to track down the Captain's paintings," was all she could say.

"Well, Vera's been calling and is worried like I am...just be ready for Friday, so I can pick you up at the airport," he said firmly.

"Okay...hey, did you get my postcard? Good, well, tell Vera that Tubby Dunbar is still here, but surely not all there. Call ya later hon, bye-bye." Rosie glanced at the clock and quickly got dressed.

Walking slowly to Valentine's, a sweaty Rosie mentally repeated her questions. She moved around to the beach side, thinking it best to tread lightly. Cleo was shaded from head to toe by an enormous umbrella. It was wind-proofed and planted in a cement block which gave her a three-hundred-sixty-degree view of the ocean and oncoming intruders. *She might think this is an invasion of privacy*, Rosie thought. *Better watch her body language…she probably wants to forget, not go tripping down memory lane.*

The newspaper headlines were shocking and half the town had been questioned, but old age can bring out the truth. Rosie's timing was right for Cleo to get it off her chest, and the story spilled out. "The Captain never got back in time for the roundup. The *Topaz* crew was arrested for extortion and murder. The drowning of the Misses and daughter was not accidental as Tiger claimed time and again. And Bull was with Mr. Amelia in Spain, copying a Goya or something, but he was still part of the plan. The investigation hit the rocks though, and there was no solid evidence—but we all knew, Tiger scammed it all for himself. Here, read this, I've saved it for years."

The headlines read, "SPORTS FISHING *TOPAZ* HOOKS MILLION-DOLLAR CATCH. AMELIA FAMILY DROWNS AT SEA."

Cleo slowly sipped an ice tea from a chilled bucket, and soon started shaking her head. "They even found out about the Lawrences, from Virginia, whose summer estate had been ransacked. Tiger sent the paintings to Europe with the Captain. He sold them in secret and made a fortune."

Rosie hadn't said a word until that point, but now she told Cleo, "Papap had a postcard from the Louvre…'Come see the Titian and Rubens, at the Ritz, Tiger.' "

"Oh yeah, he made sure of an alibi all right…slippery as an eel, but deadly as a shark," Cleo admitted. "And our little girl Josie, well, when she drowned…it was payback for all his evil deeds."

"What are you talking about?" Rosie asked. "Who's Josie?"

Cleo stood up and sauntered down to the shoreline. Minutes later she was a small red blotch sitting on a distant jetty.

Rosie started putting the bits and pieces together—she was very visual. A quick sketch with arrows pointing to the major players looked like a map of the yellow-brick road. It curved around the dead ends and liars, then got straightened out by the victims and facts. Alee and Vera would have to find out the truth sooner or later, Rosie thought. The *Topaz* fishing expeditions were not about spearing swordfish—that was just an elaborate front-the bait for the trap. *This is not just fun and games about family screw-ups,* Rosie realized. How could she explain it all to them, how his pictures from the museum visits coincided with the police discoveries of missing persons. *Wish it were a paint-by-numbers scene and not a Rubik's cube.* She made a grid-like chart to keep track of the victims. *This will make it easy to explain-show them a diagram, with who's who in Tiger's plan.* What happened to the Amelias and Lawrences was not just a lot of accidental drownings.But the bodies were never found! The Captain and crew set up the charters and played out their roles, like the boss ordered-but art fraud and cover-ups were never in their minds.

Rosie got up and turned on her heel towards Coral Key. "What a lost soul, better go and talk to Tubby Dunbar pretty quick," Rosie mumbled. "She's afraid of him too, even now, and he's old and senile...but be careful not to corner a rat, they go for the jugular."

Key West was a small, close-knit motley group of local fishermen, shopkeepers, and restaurant workers. It was easy for Tubby Dunbar and the Captain to capitalize on the parade of tourists seeking sun and fun. It was not small fry for T.D. though, he wanted what was inside the stucco mansions of old-money Southern blue-bloods. And with the Captain's help, he was going to get it one way or another.

It was barely noon when Rosie glanced out over the pristine sea and imagined the *Topaz* speeding across the straits towards the Bahamas. *Betrayal, lies, back-stabbing, and burials at sea...circling sharks,* thought Rosie, *this is way out of my league. Time to get my stuff together.* She walked back to the B & B wondering if crazy T.D. would even talk, or remember the whereabouts of any of the Captain's paintings.

Alee is never going to understand this fiasco, Rosie thought, *she just knows, like the Little Prince, that "it is only with the heart that one can see rightly, what is essential is invisible to the eye."* And Papap lost sight of the truth before she was even born. Without his art, he probably would have jumped off Long Bridge ages ago. It was greed for Tiger, but for Papap, it's not a deadly sin to copy the masters. From the porch Rosie spotted a purple-robed figure, bent down at the water's edge. *Must be the Contessa picking up spiral shells*, Rosie mused, *she's always roaming up and down in that big straw hat.*

She looked up and waved wildly at Rosie. "Heard you were look-ing for me, dearie," she yelled. "Come on over and help me dig up this conch."

"Okay, yes, hello Contessa," Rosie called out. "How are you?"

A big toothy grin and crinkled blue eyes greeted Rosie. She was glad to see a friendly face and quickly put her hand out to show respect.

Time had been washed away by the sea breezes. The presence of the Contessa, combined with the rhythm of the waves, had lulled Rosie into a quiet calm. "When I was young, guess my uncle saved us," she said softly. "My brothers and sisters came over too, from a shanty—town in Cuba. We were just teenagers, hanging on to the side of his shrimp boat. All I remember was throwing up and the hammerheads below, and wooden barrels rolling on the deck tangled in fishnets. Then we stopped on a tiny spit of land, and my uncle's friend Tiger took us and the barrels to Long Key."

Rosie listened and wanted to take out her notebook, realizing this was no fairy tale. She needed to remember the details..."The truth is in the details," the Captain used to say about the masters' technique and mysterious images, "Just tell me what you see exactly...there's a story."

"You've been here all your life?" Rosie asked feverishly.

"Well, yes, he got us all jobs with the rich folks, and my uncle stayed on the *Topaz*...they fished out of Long Key then," the Contessa explained. "Oh my, the inn is out of sight...better get back, dearie."

By the time the B & B came into view Rosie was sweating bullets. "Maybe Tubby Dunbar still has some of Papap's paintings somewhere," she suggested to the Contessa.

"You know, my dear, nobody believed that the Captain was under Tiger's thumb. He was the best artist in these parts, and handsome to boot. But then they found the Mister in Paris with him, and a lot of rolled-up paintings in their suitcases. Tiger had to rat them out, to get off," the Contessa revealed.

"What? The museum copies? Where are they?" Rosie exclaimed.

"No, no, missy, they're gone...back to New Orleans...maybe in the big house, don't know really. Oh boy, take these shells up to the porch for me, dearie? And ask Tiger about Crab Key...they fished near that cove, he's looney, you know."

Rosie shook the Contessa's hand gently. "Thank you ever so much, see you later."

"Bye-bye, it's time for a rest now," she replied.

Rosie was as anxious as the spiraling stars in Vincent Van Gogh's *Starry Night*—like springs of cosmic energy, ready to explode into sparkling bits of matter. A shower of light in the night sky-Alee's love of life combining forces with the Captain's love of art. Rosie felt their strength gathering within her-pushing her on towards the demon Tiger.

"No good calling Vera now, what do I say when I find him?" Rosie mumbled out loud. "This will make it or break it, for sure...and then I'll never see him again."

Walking past the library, Rosie saw Billy Jason eating a hotdog. She yelled hello and waved. *Wonder if he knows the Contessa...*

"How ya doin' today, Mr. Jason?" she asked.

"Mostly too tired for working; do I know you?" he asked.

"We met days ago. I'm the Captain's granddaughter, looking for his paintings and Tubby Dunbar," Rosie stated. "Hey, do you know the Contessa?"

"Everybody knows her here...she washed ashore like a mermaid," he chuckled. Rosie figured out quickly that he was truthful all right, but full of mischief, too. He still remembered the Alvarez sisters though.

The Contessa's real name was Bianca Alvarez. Her brother worked at the bait shop for Billy and T.D. Bianca and her sisters were the house maids for the Amelia and Lawrence estates. That's where she met her husband, Paolo, the caretaker. He turned out to be Tiger's ace in the hole. Spying and scheming together was a snap of the fingers, especially since the Mister and Misses went back to the Carolinas in the summer. It didn't take a mastermind to steal the original paintings and replace them with the Captain's copies while the house was empty and in the care of Paolo. The Contessa had to keep her mouth shut and help hide the money. Tiger was ruthless when it came to money; seems Paolo got in over his head and tried to stash his own pile.

He got lost on one of the out-of-town junkets and ended up in prison for five years-charged with intent to sell twenty pounds of Acapulco gold. He was almost home too-after delivering and re-hanging the rolled-up artworks. And Tiger never lifted a finger to help.

Now he was totally in charge of caretaking the estates. Bianca feared for Paolo, but mostly for herself-Tiger wouldn't take no for an answer, and she became his girlfriend. It was common knowledge that Tiger hit the jackpot—from some underwater artifacts he found and sold...so he claimed to everybody. Bianca knew he would protect his loot above all else, so she played the game. But then her little sister Tina became his next casualty-and helped destroy his own brother Dennis in the process.

Dennis and Tina were inseparable. All their late-night-into-the-morn tête-à-têtes were more than just heart-to-heart conversations. Tina became pregnant within a year. Tiger's brother Dennis was once the mayor of Long Key. He was also married with twin daughters. The brothers were partners in a popular fish and chips joint called Frutta de Mer. It was a primo hot spot located right next to the pier, alongside blazing sunsets. Bianca's kid sister, Tina, worked at night prepping in the kitchen. She was a shy, dark-haired, smoldering beauty who lived with Bianca in an apartment over the garage. But they barely saw each other.

Bianca was up and out at the crack of dawn opening up the big house. And Tina usually slept until noon.

It all started after Dennis lost his re-election. The restaurant became his second home. Once he locked eyes with Tina, her fate was sealed. Amid rumors of coke-induced all-nighters and Dennis forgetting to see his daughters and pay his bills, Tiger took over as manager. He gave Dennis an ultimatum-your family or jump ship with the girl.

Next day Tina was long gone, sent away in the dead of night. Bianca never spoke of her again, but knew she was safe-away from Tiger. It would be nine years before the sisters came face to face again. By that time Bianca had bought the Mermaid-by-the-Sea and Paolo got moved for observation at South Florida's state mental hospital. Seems he cracked up under the secrets and threats hammered down by boss Tiger.

Eventually Paolo died in his sleep, and Bianca lost her family, but time would make it right again. Tiger was away a lot on business and Tina finally came home. It was all behind the scenes for the Captain, what with his hefty museum projects and portrait studio. Sure he was dear friends with the Contessa, but she was still afraid of Tiger and kept the Captain in the dark.

"It was a fact, miss," Rosie heard Billy proclaim loudly, "the boss set us all up, but he turned like an octopus on the Captain. When it looked like he was probably going to jail, Tiger threw a shark's spear and hit Bull in the thigh...bled like a pig and nobody blinked an eye.

"Is that when he got out of town?" Rosie asked. "Leaving his paintings behind?"

"Guess so...too bad, 'cause Tiger owned most of them. Lucky he got free and not arrested," Billy said.

"You know, Mr. Jason, my grandfather was a great artist-his art hangs in a couple of museums back home," Rosie announced. "And his portraits are all over the Cape."

"Well, miss, a lot of 'em are around here too...time to scoot," Billy replied. "Go past Valentine's and see Cleo The Captain kept his studio there for a while. Oh, be careful of the nutcase in the big house, he's got more than fishnets in his closet."

Rosie hugged Billy good-bye and whispered, "Thank you from the bottom of my heart for the truth about my grandfather." She walked away with a clear-headed plan for the first time. For weeks her mixed emotions had been set adrift on a rubber raft with a needle-toothed Tiger shark circling its prey. Gray Billy Jason, a die-hard Navy man like the Captain once was, had come to her rescue. Both men were quick to right a wrong in their younger days, but then the years go by and spirits get broken. *Maybe they both still did the right thing in the end—by admitting the truth and then saving the postcards*, Rosie thought, as she walked towards Valentine's. Down the briar path she spotted an iridescent blue butterfly flitting amidst the beach roses. "Oh hello, Alee, hope you brought some pixie dust…we need it," Rosie said out loud.

Valentine's was closed until 4 pm, so Rosie went around back looking for the kitchen entrance. She stopped short; Cleo was lying on a cot, wrapped up in a white, shroud-like caftan. Her pale face, looking like a death mask, was touched up with red rouge and lipstick. The only sign of life was the labored breathing of a heavy smoker. Rosie went over and whispered, "Ms. Cleo, hello…are you sleeping?" Not a sound was heard except for the shell chimes swinging over the screen door.

Rosie walked through a large pantry and into the kitchen. She turned on the lights and across the room was a day-glo sign strip—Do Not Enter. *Not a chance* thought Rosie, and she opened the basement door. Downstairs the main room was lit by two dirty peek-a-boo windows. She pulled the chain of a hanging bulb and, blinking quickly, Rosie focused in on the walls. She turned around in a circle and gasped out loud, "It's Papap's map room…his collection of *National Geographic* maps pasted on the walls! He really was here!"

The map room was originally a Renaissance phenomenon. The illusionistic studiolo of the Duke of Urbino was a good example of how the Age of Humanism encouraged exploration of academic studies that focused on the natural world—not on God. It took the seventeenth century Age of Discovery to nail down the scientific facts of the world. Previous theories and facts of life were based on Leonardo and Galileo. The Captain's fascination with maps had been a constant dilemma for Rosie—the third-floor studio walls were covered with his own map designs. He was always sketching on top of them, colorful, wide-eyed faces of joy and surprise. Rosie never made the connection-to her it was just doodling, but more likely they were reminders of lost souls, or the faces of his friends. The maps were his memories, especially the folded map hidden in the cigar box-Alee's discovery of a lifetime.

Imagining all the universe has to offer-filling the brain with worldly images of another time and place, geography inspired every philosopher and artist from the Ancient, Medieval, and Renaissance periods, straight up to the nineteenth century with Gauguin.

Rosie was transfixed-all four walls were covered by the world. Pale blue was everywhere; even the heavy dust couldn't hide the dominating ocean areas. She zeroed in on the red crisscrosses, green squares, purple triangles, and black spirals drawn over the land masses. Rosie crept closer in order to read the message at the bottom- "around the world with Lil Josie, Capt. Papa, 4/14/23."

"What is this game?" Rosie blurted out loud. "Isles of the Blessed here, Isles of the Damned over there, the good guys versus the bad guys, maybe? Or teaching his daughter about the world!"

A map room in most cultures meant war times, but in the Renaissance, where "man is the measure of all things," it meant the search for knowledge, with universities replacing monasteries as learning centers. But still the traditional symbols, maps and Muses, were all used by the artists. After the invention of linear perspective by Brunelleschi in Florence about 1420, illusionism in art enabled us to appreciate the complexities of man and nature. The Captain just re-created their reality again, but the maps were confrontational, challenging the artist to reveal all that was new and monumental. So he journeyed with Lil Josie and played "around the world" to see all the great wonders built by human hands and minds. They went from Ancient times, to the Age of Faith and Humanism, to the Age of Discovery in a lifetime.

Rosie sat, puzzled, thinking about Lil Josie and Alee traveling to the ends of the earth through art just before the night sky covered their eyes forever. Soon a loud rattling of dishes brought her back to reality and up the stairs. No one looked twice as she slipped out the back door. Cleo was long gone, probably primping for the dinner crowd, Rosie mused. *Gotta find out about Josie...if she's still alive.* It was late afternoon by the time she reached Tiger's wrought-iron gate and looked up at the tiny windows on the roof.

Walking along the side path towards the Bay, Rosie plopped down on the stone wall. "Oh, jeez…that was Cleo in the sketchbooks nude…I remember the letters," Rosie said in amazement. "She must have been in her twenties back then, when the Captain fell in love with her."

It happened that Madam Jo died in her sleep and Cleo inherited the cabaret, and of course, a business partner-Tubby Dunbar. Being young and impressionable was not a sin, only asking for trouble, and Tiger was the older man ready to give it to her. It became too late to get out from under, and he would dominate her life or else-she wouldn't have one.While scouting future clients up north, T.D. would not be watching her every move. Cleo could be free for a while, to pose for the Captain, talk with friends, and read. Some of her favorite books were given to her by him; *Seas& Rivers of the World, Final Harvest*-Emily Dickinson's poems, *Sponges, Pearls & Sting-Rays*- Chagal's *Love Paintings* and *Wonders in the Everglades*. She had already devoured her aunts' library on alchemy,astrology, the fourth dimension, myths and legends, medieval bestiaries, and tarot tales. Cleo had been dreaming of traveling around the world with the Captain-living for months at a time in Egypt, Athens, Venice, Spain, and the Far East.

It was nearly an hour later when Rosie awoke to click-clack noises and saw the Japanese gardener scoot by on a bicycle. The Louvre could have been in ashes before she came to her senses. Her thoughts were imprisoned by the innocent, tragic lives mixed up in Tiger's schemes. Remembering Wordsworth's poem, Rosie had to "grieve not, but rather find strength in what remains behind," and beaming out of the blue— the faces of Alee, Papap, and Vera woke her up, and she walked through the garden. Hibiscus bloomed everywhere, sea grass pushed up between the flagstones on the veranda. Rosie shouted, "Hello, hello..." in through the opened French doors.

The run-down villa had once been a grand Renaissance-type palazzo like the Breakers in Newport, Rhode Island. Most of the Beaux-Arts summer "cottages" were built by Richard Morris Hunt around the turn of the century-called The Gilded Age. In the south though, plaster and stucco replaced shingle, marble, and brick, but America's richest entrepreneurs never scrimped on the fine arts. Statues, paintings, and objets d'art lavishly decorated the interiors of these faux-royal residences. But Key West had the best sunsets in the world, and it was the place where the rarest seashells and coral could be found. It also was right in the midst of a drug-infested, island-hopping paradise. Cuban cigars, swordfish, and treasure-hunting kept the *Topaz* crew busy. While the Captain Merri portrait studio was in high gear taking reservations on the pier, the rich mingled with the middle and low classes down there—all anxious to take in the screwball performers and people-watch while a sky-blue pink gave way to the red-orange fireball magically disappeared on the horizon. Ernest Hemmingway look-a-likes, wet T-shirt contests, and Tropic Tanarama girls added fuel to the nightlife. Tourists and locals fell in love with the Keys and never wanted to live anywhere else-except for Cleo and the Captain.

Part V

THE BLOOD BUCK OR
THUNDER FULL MOON

It was low tide and the beach was empty. Alongside a jetty one hunched-over figure with a dog was throwing seaweed onto the rocks. Rosie figured it was T.D. and his mutt. They dragged a skiff into the shallow waters, then rowed out and around the bend. She turned and pushed aside the salt-smeared doors. The mansion looked like an outdoor flea market—heavy drapes shut out the light, nutshells and papers littered the floor, piles of knotted rope tangled up with driftwood filled the fireplace. Rosie walked between the small stone figures and found herself staring up the grand double-staircase in the foyer, where a Palladian stained-glass window highlighted the landing. Closer inspection revealed a John LaFarge panel with the hanging wisteria, blue-violet vine pattern. She gasped out loud. "Is it possible...hidden beneath all that dirt? Probably one of his most valuable glass art works...for sure. Wonder if Mr. Amelia is here?"

Tubby and the mutt had gone over to Crab Key to check on his sponge and coral stash, leaving their clam baskets next to the jetty. She knew they were not going to be gone long and was as nervous as Alice tumbling down the rabbit's hole. That's when she saw them—two scraggly calico cats with skinny tails scampering down the hall. Most of the doors were padlocked. Her heartbeat was the only sound and its yo-yo snaps made her breathe heavily.

"Snooping around like this is crazy," Rosie mumbled. "The paintings are probably buried…or locked away somewhere…in the basement maybe."

The cats had turned the corner, disappearing behind a small door at the end of the hallway. It looked like a broom closet at first, but off to the side was a wooden staircase. Rosie peered inside and then heard tinkling noises. Her fear had turned to hope-she stepped over some mousetraps and climbed up the stairs. Dust-filled beams of light penetrated a long, narrow attic; the sounds of jingling got louder.

As her eyes adjusted to the darkened room, she saw specks of light flickering off the walls. Glass slivers crunched under her feet. Rosie stopped cold at the sight of a seated figure down at the end under a dormer window. His long white beard rested on a table amidst piles of broken glass. Suddenly he grumbled, "Did you bring the thread and glue? Hurry, Tako, here on the table."

Taken aback by his deep voice, Rosie said, "Pardon me sir…what is it? Oh my God, are you Mr. Amelia?" He didn't speak again and never knew she was there.

Dementia had set in for the old man decades ago—right after the drownings. Crushed by greed and guilt, the Mister escaped reality by having a mental breakdown. His demise was fast-Tubby Dunbar showed no mercy and banished him to the attic. Deaf and senile, the Mister lived in a jagged world, alongside his tiny matchstick figures—imprisoned in hanging glass frames, as if Picasso's Cubist portraits had come to life.

Standing next to the table, Rosie picked up one of the square prism-like creations. Sharp edges of glass pricked her thumb, drawing blood.

The miniatures could not stand up, and hundreds of them were strung along the side walls. A slight breeze creeping through the slatted windows sent them into a cacophony of twinkling jingles. Rosie felt like Pollyanna, stuck in a maze of mirrors and rainbows; dancing glass figurines dangling from the ceiling baffled the imagination.

There have always been ships-in-a-bottle, dancing puppets in glass boxes, and pears grown in sweet liquor-right on the tree. But those were delightful and fascinating. The glass hangings were full of pain and paranoia-a threatening Surrealistic nightmare fantasy.

Art is about the idea as much as the visual sensations. It becomes great art when the form equals the content; when the imagination unites them both to create a personal, new view of reality-like in the work of Van Gogh, Picasso, Dali, and now, Mr. Amelia.

Looking at the fragile miniatures, Rosie understood all of the Mister's feelings about life, people, and art. A sharp piece of glass was like a splinter—dug at and pulled out slowly, leaving scars and painful memories. How he mastered the skill with tiny sticks of wood–despite shaky hands and losing his mind—was incomprehensible to Rosie. Like Rembrandt's eyes in his self-portraits, expressing his being, these were Mr. Amelia's eyes and the "windows of his soul."

Aroused by barking and banging, Rosie beat feet to the stairs. From the hallway window, she saw Tiger hitting the stone wall with his cane—shells flying everywhere. Light raking across the landing caught her by surprise. The sheets hanging along the walls were torn at the top-held by a few threads. The weight from dirt and time had pulled them down, leaving large gaping holes. What Rosie saw hidden underneath them was a near miracle.

The gilded frames caught the light and dazzled like sparklers. All the way down the stairs she could see the tops of the frames. In an instant, Rosie yanked on the sheet-falling and scattering dust filled the air—and it landed in a heap on the stairs. The Amelia art collection would have rivaled the Prado, only these were master reproductions! Rosie stood paralyzed-electric shock paddles couldn't have jump-started her brain at that point. Even in low light, the paintings were colorful, vibrant, and breathtaking; Ruben's *Garden of Love*, Velasquez's *Las Meninas*, Caravaggio's *Bacchus* and Manet's *Bar at the Folies Bergere*.

"Oh my God...the Captain's copies! Right here, in the flesh. I don't believe it!"

She walked slowly down the stairs in awe at the flawless renderings of the fakes. The Captain had truly become a genius-master for a while, feeling and understanding the meaning of greatness. Two small, double-hung works froze Rosie at the bottom of the stairs—Vermeer's *Concert* and Rembrandt's *The Mill*.

"Those paintings were stolen from the Gardner decades ago," she exclaimed. "What are they doing here?"

"Did Papap copy those too? They couldn't be the real thing!"

The Gardner heist took place more than fifteen years ago-one of the biggest art thefts ever committed. Over 200 million dollars' worth of art was stolen by locals dressed up as cops, who gained entry and then tied up the security guards. They stole thirteen priceless paintings and drawings-cut them right out of their frames. And they've never been found.

The Captain's labors of love were perfect reproductions. They gave him a taste of glory and a way to pay the highest honor and respect to his master-gods. Forgeries were big business and big trouble-only infrared x-rays could reveal the truth; unless Tubby Dunbar was in on the action -he'd know if it was a copy or not.

Rosie jammed the drapes back to get a better look. Faces, gestures, sensual nudes, and dramatic light effects looked like they could have been painted yesterday. She felt like Howard Carter discovering King Tut's tomb, "gold, gold, everywhere..." and then the curse arrived; not the mummy's curse but Tubby Dunbar screaming around the corner, "Hey, what are you doing there?" Rosie saw him rushing up the stairs yelling, "You're lookin' for trouble, missy."

She yelled back at him, "Just wait...stop...these are my grandfather's paintings, you stole them!"

"He got paid in spades for them," he snarled.

"You mean blood money, don't you?" she shot back.

"You gotta go...now," he stammered. Then, lifting his cane up towards Rosie and losing his balance, he fell back hard against the railing-tumbling down the stairs. The mutt was first to run over, sniffing and licking his face. Seconds later he was howling like a wolf at the moon. Rosie stood back waiting for signs of life, but Dunbar's eyes were closed. Terrified and shaky, she bent over him to see if he was breathing. His eyes snapped open and he gasped for air; Rosie heard only one word, "boathouse" and he then died-of a rotten heart and old age. His pock-marked face looked like a beat-up, desiccated rubber mask.

Rosie was still kneeling down when the old gardener came in to see about the commotion. She jumped up in a tizzy. "He's dead, probably a heart attack, I'm going to go and get the police."

"No, no," he cut her off short and put his hands up. "They will take us all away," he cried.

"Okay, it's all right, I understand...then I'll come back tomorrow..." she said nervously.

Bowing slowly to her, he nodded and grabbed both her hands in a surprising gesture of many thanks.

Spaced out and scared, Rosie saw nothing on her way back to the Mermaid Inn. She sat on her bed in a mental state of ping-pong. "To turn the world upside down or in good conscience-do nothing." The dilemma was resolved by a ringing telephone breaking her concentration-making it easier to just let it go for everybody's sake. It was Vera. "Been calling you for days, Rose...Alee and me are going crazy. You coming home tomorrow?"

"Hold on Vera, Papap's copies are here...and Tubby Dunbar is gone... a couple more days and I'll tell you then, just make sure Alee knows we did it," Rosie said calmly. "Tell her to study Picasso's *Guernica*-to see what war is like."

The raspy voice of T.D. echoed in her brain; "boathouse" was branded there forever. *Can't even feel sorry for the old coot...no telling what the deal is with the boathouse,* Rosie pondered. Sleeping was next to impossible with moon-eyed Alee skipping through her mind. It was her trust and kindness compared to the lying and cheating sociopaths that bewildered her the most. People sharing the same world, where at any time or any place innocence and goodness can be crushed. Alee personified the heart, pride, and spirit once possessed by humankind, similar to the ancient Greek statuary that portrayed character and principles in the ideal perfection of the body and mind. Human weakness today makes us victims, not masters of our destiny. We are bombarded and tempted by the get-rich-quick scams. The seven deadly sins are coming back to haunt us-like in the Hell panel by Bosch. The miser excretes coins for greed and the sodomite is shot with an arrow for lust.

Alee was spared the corruption, but not the pollution of the world. She'll be forever young, always a guardian angel, never a mere mortal. One of William Blake's maidens caught up in the *Whirlwind of Lovers* constant spiral of embracing couples—denied true love by fate. Blake's poetry added to his hand-colored prints created the imagined, joyful world that Alee knew before her cancer hit. Like in his poems; "Tyger, Tyger burning bright, in the forests of the night..." or Vera's favorite of all—"to see the world in a grain of sand....And heaven in a wild flower, hold eternity in the palm of your hand..."

It was still dark outside when Rosie awoke. Dawn was on the horizon, but the full Beaver moon kept her company as she walked silently through town. Drunken early morning partiers were heard laughing loudly nearby, but she had tunnel vision all the way to the Amelia's.

The gardener buried T.D. amidst the weeds with only a piece of driftwood to mark the grave—"Tiberius Dunbar 1901-1989." He had no friends or family to notify, only his Irish wolfhound was there digging like a mad dog all around the grave.

Going down to the boathouse was not foremost in Rosie's mind, but the fate of the copies was crucial. The phone call to Vera shook her back to reality-there was no legal claim to the paintings. She was going to have to leave them. These priceless artworks of Velasquez, Rubens, Rembrandt, Matisse…it was as close as she would ever get to the real thing! Papap used to say, "Experience the artists' ideas made visible…ideas of truth and beauty, and you will understand, Rosie." Imagining her grandfather in the museum, painting the secrets of the masters and feeling like he was Michelangelo for a day, was, for Rosie, the legacy he gave to his family.

Alee should have had a bite out of the apple in Paradise, and seen Nature's wonders and creatures. Instead she listened to Rosie's history lessons about how great art and Papap were the best teachers in the world. It was easy to imagine those two sitting side by side in the Louvre-the angelic muse and the artist 'terribilta.'

The stucco mansion, all decked out by the moonlight, shone bright that night, as if released from a tyrant. It seemed like the middle of the day to Rosie, and she was invited to view the Royal Collection in the Prado, where she explored and contemplated traditional myths and stories about human nature. "Now I know why the Mona Lisa is smiling," Rosie whispered, "she's secretly guarding all the mysterious forces of nature festering behind her—keeping the humans away, before they corrupt and pollute it all." True, she dominates the landscape in a monumental way, but that sfumato and mix of acid greens, smoldering browns, and gray suggest a hostile world. "Those majestic copies were born out love and respect, not malice or deceit by the Captain," Rosie sighed, "they should live on and be appreciated now. Maybe even donate them to my old art school, to be used for discussion on the techniques and iconography used by the artists."

Like the aurora borealis, star-struck and mind ablaze, Rosie went up and down with a searchlight, taking pictures with a cheap, flash camera. "Alee and Vera have got to see these paintings close up, else they'll never understand why Papap risked it all," Rosie concluded. "Illusions of grandeur blinded his judgment, but then losing touch with the reality of the scam was his salvation for sure!"

The aesthetic high was inspirational enough for the Captain—no match, though, against his inevitable fall from grace—evil wrongdoings flow fast and furious over good intentions; bad karma and all. The Captain was a major player in Tiger's bait and switch, but the so-called accidental drownings broke his heart and spirit. Leaving Key West, Valentine's, and his beloved copies behind was what kept him alive another forty years. His museum stories were true enough, but he had never told Rosie about any master reproductions, only about his own art; especially his many seaside-pirate murals all over the Cape.

Royal was yelping upstairs somewhere. *Hanging around Mr. Amelia most likely, wonder what will happen to him,* Rosie mused, as she glanced across the bay. *Now it's up to the gardener…he's been the caretaker anyway. Wait till they find out about the collection: the estate's value could double and knock the art world for a loop with Tiger down for the dirt nap.*

The surface of the sea looked like one of the facets on the Hope Diamond. A sublime ocean of infinite beauty—hiding its destructive forces and dead bodies. Like in the classical myths-omnificent Zeus rules the heavens, Neptune steers us into a watery realm and Hades burns us to ashes while the chosen angels take flight. *Be good, be bad, what does it matter in the end-we all end up dead,* Rosie pondered. *Art makes the world come alive and distracts the gods for a while. Making life beautiful for as long as possible-that was Papap's code. Guess he did the best he could for the ones he loved and lost.*

It was dusk when Rosie set off down the beach to find the boathouse. The pathway from the back side of the manse had been overgrown for years, so Rosie went the long way-past the jetty and around the bend. The pointed, cone-shaped roof came into view soon enough, despite the tall, purple-topped sea grass hiding the shingles. A couple of battered dinghies lay tied up with nets nearby, while broken pieces of red coral and worm-holed sponges led up to a door.

Rosie felt goose bumps and sweat beads on her upper lip, but she kept on walking. She shook off the pins and needles in her hands. The mutt was digging in the sand down at the water's edge. It was low tide and there were plenty of clam holes and sandpipers pecking here and there-suddenly Rosie stopped dead in her tracks. A full, pink-orange moon rose up on the horizon. Her sense of wonder was overwhelming and ominous at the same time. Even Leonardo's primeval landscapes never communicated the vast mysteries of creation better than Mother Nature herself. At that moment, Rosie was as calm and confident as Michelangelo's *David*-knowing that art and life are intimate partners. That we live in a Pandora's box of truth, beauty, tragedy, and death; all the timeless subjects and ideas explored by ancient philosophers and great artists.

Rosie pushed open the door. It didn't look like a boathouse, more like a shrine. In the center of the room was a white marble statue-similar to the Hans Christian Anderson's *Little Mermaid* in the harbor at

Copenhagen, only this girl held a conch shell with water flowing down into a pool at her feet. Round sea pebbles in the water spelled out the name "Lil Josie." She was a fountain of pure joy! Marble crystals picked up the moonlight and flickering candles highlighted her face. Mesmerized, thinking of Alee, Rosie couldn't believe the resemblance-it was uncanny for sure…but not for distant cousins.

Without hesitation Rosie exclaimed, "Lil Josie and Alee are family! Papap had another daughter! Oh my God…is it true?

"Oh yeah, yeah, she was Captain Merri's little girl," a deep, mono-tone voice came out of the far corner. "And she still lives here."

"What are you doing over there?" Rosie inquired.

"My name is Tako…I sleep here," the gardener said slowly, "with Lil Jo."

Tako Kataoka had been Mr. Amelia's gardener most of his seventy years. He kept the old man alive and watched the world go by. That is, until the death of Tubby Dunbar. Seeing death can make us all want to go to confession, and Tako was no different. His eyes were dark and his face more like a sad Kabuki mask than flesh and blood. Keeping silent with deadly secrets was his only regret. Now he was free and felt like talking….sharing his memories.

"Please tell me, really…who is Lil Jo?" Rosie begged.

"Miss Cleo's baby girl…and the Captain's too. He loved to paint them both. But that was a big problem, 'cause he always went away and boss Tiger thought he was daddy. Miss Cleo was a teenager, I think, but her eyes and heart beat for him. Their secret lasted many years. Right up until the little one went under the sea to live."

Rosie stared through the candlelight at the gardener's face. His soft-spoken voice was hypnotic. She hadn't begun to process all the revela-tions-with her eyes burning and Alee's face carved big-as-life, as Josie-lives intertwined here and now. Same blood, same statue, same innocence-like the woven Tree of Life mandala, or great master plan of family and Mother Nature.

Moonlight shot through the tall, bare windows and the walls became visible. Hanging nets held a collage of glass buoys, broken whelks, starfish and bits of brain coral. A startling array of natural phenomena arranged Zen-like for contemplating life and beauty. Puzzled at the textures and shapes, Rosie stood up for a closer look.

"Don't go yet, dearie," the gardener ordered, "she'll be here soon to play with her friends…Josie doesn't like the beach anymore." Rosie couldn't leave even if she wanted to-Tako was starting to ramble.

"It was late winter when Mother Nature sent two of her rarest warnings-premonitions of tragedy: a silvery blue moon in December and a killer red tide in early January. The Captain had been painting for months in Spain, living with clients in a villa outside Madrid. It was easy for Tiger to take care of Lil Josie and Cleo-they lived with his silent partner-Madam Jo. Josie usually played on the dock, watching the *Topaz* crew bring in the daily catch. She even jumped in to snatch up shells and starfish from the shallow waters. Tiger's tiny mermaid was the only true joy in his life.

"Josie came running up to the house that day, screaming about blood on the beach. Tiger scooped her up and held her tight-patting her hair as he walked back to check it out. He bent down with her to see clumps of seaweed crawling with bright red ant-like organisms. All the leaves and stems had been eaten into by the spreading fungus. Josie stopped crying after a while, but wouldn't go near the beach again."

It seemed like hours before Tako stopped talking-the only time Rosie interrupted him was when he said, "It was a blooming fungus." She jolted upright, exclaiming, " Mold, virus, bacteria…. Mother Nature can be so cruel, she has so many ways to kill us.!"

"It was only a couple weeks later when Tiger took her over to Sanibel Isle for mother-of-pearl and spiral shells," Tako continued. "The whaler had been pulled up onto the beach. Josie set her blue plastic buckets inside and decided to run in for a swim. Tiger had been waving from a short distance away, but by the time he got to the boat she was adrift; the current carried her too far out and the undertow took her down. Her head never came up for air again. Tiger sat in disbelief aboard the Coast Guard ship-after a four-day search, they said she accidentally drowned."

The gardener had blown out the candles just before dawn. He smoothed out his coverlet and silently waved good-bye to Lil Jo and Rosie. She watched through the windows as he walked towards the sea, until red dancing figures caught her eye. Rosie was thunderstruck-hiding under the netting, hanging on the wall, was an array of friends painted for Lil Josie! The Captain's master reproductions of the Fathers of Modern Art—Matisse's *The Dance*, Rousseau's *The Dream*, Picasso's *Girl Before a Mirror*, Chagall's *Lovers with Birds*, and Gauguin's *Tahitian Girl*. Lil Josie's companions, amusing her and speaking to her day and night. Watching from behind the door was Miro's *Clown Maestro* from the Harlequins' Carnival-a most delightful and disturbing creature for sure,with needle-like arms waving up and down, surrounding a sad, sinister red-blue face.

Rosie felt liquid gold running through her veins. Imagine her and Alee playing with them while the Captain was away, making sure his Lil Josie was surrounded by as much stimulating images as possible. Everything to satisfy the curiosity of a child, and to distract her from all the unexplained, random acts in life and death. The songbirds still sing every year, but there's nothing fair about Mother Nature's game plan. The rules are always changing, except for the basic ones-the good die young and the cheaters live the longest. Rosie smiled back at the white, ghostly image of Lil Josie and thought about home and Alee. "Bye-bye sweetheart...here's your heaven on earth with all your buddies around-where Papa gave you his love," she whispered.

The way back to the inn was at least a three to four mile stretch along the beach. It could have been longer; it didn't matter to Rosie. It was more important to know the convoluted truth, and to put the copies behind her--they would only be misunderstood.

Leaving Key West in the morning was a relief and broke her heart at the same time. She took no souvenirs, except for a chunk of red coral and a pink-covered sketchbook the gardener gave her in the boathouse. She never saw the copies again; perhaps they got sold at an auction.

Alee and Vera stood on the curb waiting for Rosie to arrive.

"Hey, hey, over here, sis," Vera yelled. "Run and get her, Alee." Rosie looked around and saw Alee skipping towards her with a beaming smile-big enough to stop traffic.

"Hello honey, what a great surprise, ...where's Sean?" Rosie asked as she hugged her too tight.

"We called him last night and begged him to let us come and get you," Alee giggled. "What'd ya find out, Aunt Rosie?"

"It was like a lost Paradise, Alee...lots of the Captain's friends had died, there was an empty sea and sky for miles, but Papap's paintings were alive and glorious. Oh, and here's another sketchbook with your cousins' photos pasted in it."

While Vera focused on driving in traffic, Alee sat in the back, thoughtfully looking at the sketchbook. Rosie felt the time slipping away, but if the truth be told, there should have been more questions than answers. *To speak ill of the dead now is more of the same; back-stabbing like Tubby Dunbar did*, thought Rosie. She expected an onslaught of who, what, and why, but Alee and Vera really didn't know what to ask...except, "Did you bring the map back?"

Soon they would be over the bridge. Rosie stayed quietly calm. It was a journey of discovery she would never forget-Alee and Vera imagined it as a fantastic adventure or murder mystery, but she thanked her lucky stars every day for the love of Alee and Papap, and for the chance to find out the truth.

"Here's the map and postcards, Alee...it all worked out," Rosie smiled. "And look at these family trees I made last night for you too. Down at the bottom is a list of Papap's paintings...you know most of them already from the text. They all tell stories about his life and and the artists he loved."

"Oh no, Aunt Rosie, these can't be Papap's," Alee stated.

"Well, yes they are, Alee, master copies of all his favorites-full of beauty and tragedy. And you had a cousin, Lil Josie, there's a statue of her looking just like you. She drowned really young. Read the names on the branches...many people drowned down there...maybe, as sacrificial victims to the sea gods- who knows what's an accident or just bad luck....."

Every so often Vera would glance at Rosie with a look of understanding-knowing that they were a part of Alee's roller-coaster ride of her life-short, fast, and exhilarating. Sisters and best friends, Rosie and Vera sat quiet-there was plenty of time later for a heart-to-heart.

As always, Rosie looked down both sides of the canal, gazing at the Buzzards Bay railroad bridge, the last of its kind on the east coast. She remembered how the Captain loved to say, "Great art makes life and ideas visible...read the symbols and feel the colors." But then as she watched Alee's fascination over the names, sketches, and tiny photos, another "simple secret" came to mind, her favorite pearl of wisdom from the Little Prince: "It's only with the heart that one can see rightly...what is essential is invisible to the eye." Alee already knew that, of course, that's how it all began up in the Captain's studio-asking why he loved art so much.

The weeks passed quicker than one of Alee's back-spins. March came blowing in with warming winds across Vineyard Sound, while the squid boats fished offshore. In a month or so everybody would be clamoring for a seat on the deck, and the Happy Hour specials. The Club was famous for the afternoon ritual-sipping cold beer and downing shots of Cuervo gold. Smelling lime over salty fingers and feeling warm all over marked the official start of summer on the Cape.

Alee was nearly eleven years old that summer following the Key West excursion into Tiger's shark den. Then, in early August, it happened shortly after sunrise-the Heights looked like an ocean on the Red Planet. The spreading red algae was more toxic than an oil spill. The oozing, iridescent surface was just as infectious and fatal as a bluefish bite. The bizarre phenomena even perplexed the bug hunters at the Marine Labs-

not even their horseshoe crab studies came before it. The scientists claimed it was one of Mother Nature's untimely mix of temperature, bacteria, and tides. It all added up to killer pathogens contaminating shellfish and marine life. Endless tests by researchers at the Woods Hole Oceanographic Institute, or WHOI, struggled to solve the dilemma of a red tide-but it was as random and destructive as cancer.

Rosie and Vera came to work on time that morning. As they walked through the empty restaurant they heard Lily yelling from the office, "Get off the beach, Alee...oh no, where's Grandpap?"

"Hey Lily, what's the matter?" Vera hollered.

"Go out to the deck and find Daddy," she replied. "Hurry up."

Rosie had heard about it before,remembering the words,' blood on the beach'. "No Vera, the water's not on fire-it's a red tide...better get down to the jetty, tell Dad and Alee not to go near the seaweed." Rosie watched her father scoop up Alee in his arms and look out to sea.

The Baron, as his employees called him, had been checking the tide charts for his bluefish trip, when he saw the glowing clumps of seaweed floating across the surface. Pat Merrick had looked upon that part of Vineyard Sound for thirty years. Not once had he ever seen it become a slow-moving field of lava-heading straight for the deck. Truly it was a freak of nature-thousands of fiery, furry-like microscopic organisms eating and multiplying into tiny blooms of algae. Rosie looked out across the Sound and saw her father and Alee hugging each other on the jetty. The blanket of red-orange seaweed reminded Rosie of the sky in the background of Edvard Munch's *The Scream*-with the terrifying, blood-red clouds swarming and echoing his fears of open spaces, as he stands alone on a bridge.

Like Alee's infection, lying dormant until it strikes at will, her blood teeming with cells that lost their way, the red tide rapidly spreads and kills. Running to catch up with her grandfather on the jetty was a symbolic twist of fate on Alee's future of only two years. The red tide was short-lived too. It went out with the next high tide, but the Bud Moon rising up from the horizon was a blood-orange too.

That was the summer of '73 and the Captain began painting his murals in the downstairs bar. Rosie got her first art internship that year, assisting her Papap—mixing the pigments, preparing the gesso, cleaning brushes, and applying the varnish. It was a good thing too, because in a couple of years she would be accepted at Mass Art in Boston. Not for her painting skills but as a fiber artist; taking weaving classes. The wall hangings and tapestries got her into the prestigious, state-funded art school—right at a time in her life when choices were crucial, life-altering even.

Rosie was a borderline hippie, just after the '60s. Individualism was pursued, but the impulse to stay and get married was pulling harder. The Captain used to say, "Small towns, small minds," but it was more like, "Be safe and secure...work in the family business." Choices are a kind of freedom to do what you want, not what somebody else wants you to do...so she went over the bridge and never looked back. It was the only chance to get a life of her own and learn about the world. *To be knowledgeable and become an expert in one area—that's how you get respect and self-esteem*, Rosie thought. And it took years-ten years—to feel that pride and fulfillment. As she watched the Captain prepare the wall for his paintings—Woods Hole, New Bedford, Gay Head, and Nobska—never once did she realize how important and great he truly was...and how the summers of Alee skipping in and out of the dark downstairs into the sunlight would be the happiest days of her life.

Alee collected many scallop and jingle shells with her Papap in front of the deck, when he wasn't out fishing. They even made a bizarre shell ceiling with a bright red background in the restaurant. Not really natural and attractive, more like bold and aggressive. Guess that's what the Baron had in mind the afternoon he moored just off shore; to show off his fishing expertise of course, but to also bring in a powerful catch-of-the-day—for all to behold.

Rosie and Vera were working the late lunch crowd, and Lily was getting ready to go to the bank. When the engines got louder and Alee ran down the stairs towards the shore yelling and waving, all eyes turned to see the action. Lily even got on the phone; "Mom, better get down here, Dad's filling up the dinghies with sharks." Everything stopped; the kids came running down the beach, the cocktailers put down their drinks and stood up against the railing; Rosie leaned over to whisper to Lily, "This is better than cable, and look at the crowd."

At one time before the hurricane of '38 the Cottage Club had its own dock with people sitting side by side, swishing their toes in the water. The old black-and-white photos from 1923 hanging in the entranceway of the Club showed a history of fashionable people. There was a small private beach—club property, where boats, dogs, dancing, and drinking were allowed. Now the Baron had his own bright yellow boat mooring where the dock once jutted into the sea. The restaurant was famous for its "Bluefish all-you-can-eat Wednesday night special." The thirty-two-foot sports-fishing cruiser was impressive, but the tubs of fish the Baron and his crew caught in an afternoon were shocking. Most of the days it was all bluefish—those fighting, oily, dark-flesh fillets that native Cape Codders relished. The bass were scarce and threatened—banned from summer menus for years.

On this late afternoon, it was only blue and mako sharks that spilled out of the rowboats. The kitchen help came running out the back door in their shorts to swim out with ropes and fish tubs. Then the Baron shouted orders to his crew: "Pull in the boats, spear 'em, hurry and load them up." All you could see from the deck were the huge tail fins sticking out, piled on top of one another. The sharks were too heavy, and many a dinghy sank from the weight—lucky they were attached to ropes, or instead of lying on the shore they'd be lost on the bottom of Vineyard Sound.

Phelia came pushing her way out onto the deck and said, "Hey you two, what's all the fuss about?" Rosie and Lily grabbed her. "Mom, you've never seen this before." The beach had cleared out, kids jumped and squealed about, and Alee stood firm—she turned to look up at her mother, and for all of us, a moment of love and pride was etched on our faces forever.

An instantaneous Kodak family moment-that's what Pat Merrick gave his family and made it all worthwhile. But on this day he gave everybody a sense of wonder and awe—for one of Nature's most ruthless, efficient killing machines. At least twenty-five enormous, gray-skinned streamlined sharks lay on the beach—all gutted with their bellies hanging open. Rows and rows of white, needle-sharp teeth lined the gaping jaws of these monsters. Alee was right up front poking and touching fearlessly inside and out. One of the kids ran off screaming for help—Rosie looked around to see wide-eyed, open-mouthed spectators everywhere. "Gotta get down there and get a close-up view. Grab Alee for me," Lily said. Just to see a dead shark was a thrilling experience, the closest any of us would ever get to one and live. In the restaurant, first-timers would be taken aback just by seeing the bleached jawbones of a shark hanging here and there from the rafters-let alone touch one.

Rosie even made earrings and a heishe shark-tooth necklace from a jar of teeth the Baron kept on his desk. That day was one of the Baron's most crowning moments. His family watched and waved to him from the deck-feeling as famous and proud as the figures in Raphael's Vatican frescoes from the High Renaissance.

As a fisherman, the Baron was a maniac. Vera swore she'd never go out with him again—after the time she threw up for three hours straight and all she heard was, "Ha, ha, you'll be all right soon..." but he never turned back. Mark, the oldest son, and Teddy, Vera's husband, went out every week to catch bluefish with him. Going far out to the canyon was an ordeal. Teddy flinched every time he saw the Baron after the "freeze" incident-he would gesture instead of saying hello, because Teddy's arms had cramped up in the chair after hours of pulling in blues. The paralyzing pain from his shoulder and arm muscles had been worse than ten pinched nerves. The Baron joked about it all summer-but Teddy still became one of his best fishing buddies.

Teddy went with the Baron to the last hockey game in Newport; to see the grandkids play. The weekend tournament was nearly over when his heart attack struck, as fast as a shark chomping off a leg—and Pat Merrick died in an instant. Seems the doctor had been telling him for months to stay out of the cold, since it constricts the heart muscles. Teddy even commented one night as they were getting ready to go to dinner, "Jeez, Pat, it's a hundred degrees in here."

"That's okay, it's comfortable for me," he replied. Some warning signals for sure, but it had been more than ten years since the Baron had his quadruple by-pass heart surgery-guess his time was up.

Like the Captain loved painting, the Baron's greatest thrill was battling the winds and the tides, and catching all those free fish for his restaurant—he had a sign on his desk saying "I fish therefore I am." A Shakespearean scholar he was not, but a profound love of the game and a dry, quick wit were in his blood nonetheless.

The murals were painted that summer of '73 and business could not have been better. The heyday of Happy Hours and Rock and Roll was on the beach at the Cottage Club. Wet T-shirt contests, Hawaiian Tropic models selling lotion in skimpy bikinis parading about...along with the notorious jello contest and mud-wrestling in plastic swimming pools. Of course, when the drunken participants got all fired up from the crowd and music and their bathing suits fell down around their ankles-it nearly became sex on the beach! Just in the nick of time though, the Baron cut the lights and the show was over—before the cops arrived to round up the drunk and disorderly. It was one of his major coups—no arrests, no fines, only the sound of *ca-ching, ca-ching* on the registers. *Cape Cod* magazine gave it the "most popular bar on the Cape" award for nearly a decade-Pat Merrick had built his castle-by-the-sea.

Rosie, her sisters, and her brothers, Mark and Brian, felt set for life. They always had jobs at the Club. It was the Baron's way of establishing a sense of family togetherness at work. He made it lucrative, secure, and easy for his kids to have a big-shot lifestyle-with money to burn and rivers of champagne to drown in. The restaurant was old and in disrepair for sure, but the location and collection of nautical paintings and photos added a rustic, marine atmosphere. He even had a moose head joining the dinner crowd! The Captain walked around touching up murals and sketching tourists, giving the place authenticity. Seaside quaint and breezy by day, Beaver Brown and Whitey Wonders at night made it easy to sing that "these were the days my friend…that would never end"…and life would be like this forever."

Painting his New England murals that summer, the Captain often looked like the old man of the sea-wearing a beret. With only a few brushstrokes, free-formed shapes turned into brightly colored figures that carried the eye through the boating and swimming scenes. He painted quickly in a linear style, outlining bodies and faces. His work was similar to the bold, flat shapes and clashing colors of French expressionism-a style called Fauvism or the "wild beasts." The iconography was second to their avant-garde, explosive designs. Dufy, Matisse, and Derain taught the Captain technique first, and then a radical, 'art is what you make it'.

Rosie just listened as she hung around, cleaning up paint splatters and brushes. "Frescoes and wall paintings have a long history, dearie," said the Captain. "Murals allow the artist to create on a monumental scale, yeah, for decorations sometimes…but mostly they reflect ideas about life and pictures of people laughing and crying…" Getting the bar set up for the night usually interrupted, cutting short his sessions. Before long Rosie got the art history lecture of her life…and she never forgot the trance-like look on his face, as if he were time-warping into another zone.

"You've seen the cave paintings–a variety of majestic animals thundering across the ceiling?" he asked. "Well, those artists fulfilled a survival need and ritualized the hunt to ensure success—to eat. That's the greatest art of all, when form and content are one.

"And the Egyptians depicted all their beliefs—gods and goddesses, family life of the Royals, and mummification practices. Tut, Ra, Ramses, Isis, Osiris-frescoes and sculptures depicting stories of Egyptian life and death.

We learn about these ancient cultures through their artwork. Like the Romans...who decorated palazzos and villas with frescoes. Landscapes, still-life, portraits, and pagan rituals in a totally natural, yet illusionistic style—the Roman artists were great at giving the impression of looking out a window into light and space. They created such masterpieces that the Renaissance masters looked back to them for inspiration. Leonardo, Michelangelo, and Raphael gave birth to the High Renaissance style about 1500. *The Last Supper*, the Sistine Ceiling, and Raphael's *Stanze della Segnatura* frescoes, especially his School Of Athens-all were a revival of classical forms and ideas from Greece and Rome."

Rosie was as curious as a goldfish in a bowl, eyes darting here and there; he had triggered a spark and she was hooked. He reeled her in all summer long with his art tales. The Captain kept painting while he talked to Rosie and before she knew it, the blank, blue wall was covered with loosely sketched people, boats, and islands. Names of towns and signs were written along the bottom—not telling serious stories, more like a series of personal and delightful genre scenes. His portrayal of everyday life by the sea; a visual and verbal explanation of Cape Cod harbors, road races, regattas, and local clam shacks magically appearing out of the blue.

The Club murals were his last artworks—Rosie found her Papap right after Thanksgiving, stone-cold, wrapped in an old quilt, up in the attic studio. The dampness had crept right into his bones, and he died of pneumonia that year at the age of eighty-two. That was the first time she ever saw Tubby Dunbar—at the funeral, a decrepit, hunched-over figure walking across a sunlit field.

A scali cap covered his eyes and he spoke to no one. After he pushed a pile of dirt into the grave, he scuffled back to a waiting taxi. Rosie never had a clue that he was her Papap's evil twin-partner. She kicked herself for not talking to him and asking him about his buddy. Rosie thought the Captain's legacy would be his paintings-not his Bull Merrick notoriety. His master fakes showed the ultimate respect; but only a precious few knew his philosophy. Rosie heard it: "Nature creates and art communicates. It's Nature's grandeur that is the Higher Power-revealing a profound spirituality inspiring all of us. Either we create art to immortalize her or to understand ourselves." It was then she realized he loved art more then himself.

It was only a year or so later when Alee pleaded and puzzled over the frayed treasure map...when the studio became her family swan-song. Learning about the *Ut pictura poesis* in art-how painting and poetry become one—was the grand finale. She was that young maiden in the Black Forest looking up at the long white-haired troll pointing a finger. "Beauty and wisdom are rare for one so young to wear; we look every-where for a lifetime for the key; when all along she dwells by the sea."

Pat Merrick was the king of the Cottage Club, ruling over his family like an absolute monarch. Only he earned his title the hard way-working day and night at two jobs. By the age of sixty he had became a self-made millionaire. His vending-machine business was the key to his success…and that's how he met Hank McCann. The Worcester businessman was tired and ready to sell his restaurant. Pat Merrick came in to fill the cigarette machine one day, and left with a five-year contract and the option to buy. Pat was only forty-nine years old when he moved his large family to the seaside town of Falmouth-way over the bridge.

As Rosie watched her father's triumphant return from the canyon with a boatload of sharks one day, she thought about how the Sun King took his grand walk down the Hall of Mirrors at Versailles. It was a glorious sight for his entourage to witness-Louis XIV as Apollo reborn. The Baron was waving from the top of the cruiser at his Phelia, who stood grinning next to her daughters on the deck. Lily snapped photos of the scene and all the kids ran down to the beach.

Both of his sons, Mark and Brian, worked at the Club for over twenty years and never got more than a manager title...and a love-hate relationship with each other. The Baron should have gotten a tattoo on his chest: "my castle, my money, my fish" and let the boys stop hoping for financial responsibility. With Pat Merrick you knew your place... and it was never any higher than himself-Napoleon complex or not. He wasn't a puppet-master per se, only a father expecting too much from his sons-pretending they could have a piece of the action someday. They had it made anyway—fast money, instant popularity, and a bartending job to kill for. It wasn't the sex and rock and roll that eventually did them in-it was the booze and late-night partying. "And you think you can run this place?" the Baron would shout every other day. "Try getting up in the morning first."

The time came when Mark had had enough-he got a loan to start his own restaurant, a Mexican cantina just down the road. The tequila flowed along with the nachos grande-washed down with Corona and Dos Equis. Brian even went with him to help manage and bartend. The years went rolling right by-until the taxes and bills started piling up.

Too many after-hour drinks turned into early morning hangovers-going to bed at thirty-five but waking up looking like fifty-five took its toll. Even watching the sunrise was painful, especially with the sound of squawking gulls gathering on the beach. Oh yes, and the drive home was like one big guilt trip-fried, toasted, and broiled was a better description of the bar owners, not the fish on the menu. Not to mention the dessert-that was the best part, finishing the duck sauce until it was all gone. Rosie had been there, done that, and got the T-shirt summer after summer, enough times that it became old and boring.

One of the last summers her mother was alive, Rosie thankfully found a new best friend-her mother, Phelia. No more nights of partying until daybreak and buzzing home just before her father got up to go fishing. No more tip-toeing down the hallway and wondering if she should flush the toilet-so as not to wake them up. It was such a drag to keep saying, "Do they know what I've been doing all night...Hope they don't think I was having sex all night." Rosie liked intellectual stimulation way before the physical kind. The guilt would pass after an hour or two, and before long her mother would peek in and say, "Wake up, sleepy head, let's go for breakfast...boy, it smells like booze in here." "Okay, okay, Ma, open a window," Rosie would reply, laughing inside. "I'll jump in the shower, give me fifteen minutes."

Phelia's last years and the Baron's run of thirty years owning the club coincided with the best times in Rosie's life. Weekends hanging out with Phelia, watching movies, shopping and eating wiener schnitzel and fettuccine at the Golden Swan were their favorites. Her mother was funny, generous, and remarkably blunt to a fault. She loved to jack up the volume on her Ella Fitzgerald and Frank Sinatra songs on her ride down to the restaurant.

Everybody felt comfortable talking to Phelia about most anything, from allergies to crossword puzzles, seven-letter scrabble words to true-life murder mysteries.

There was one lesson Rosie never forgot, and years later she came to understand her mother's outburst. They sat at the Cantina one late afternoon eating quesadillas and sipping frozen margaritas. "Look, Rosie, parents help the kids that need it most; you're in school and can take care of yourself," Phelia stated. "But what did they do to make you proud, Ma?" Rosie shot back.

It sounded so unfair to her at the time...but she dropped the subject anyway. Those words still rang in Rosie's ears, a decade later-how she learned about a mother's unconditional love. Surviving the sex, drugs, and rock and roll was just plain lucky, compared to the good fortune and character she inherited from her parents.

As a teacher in several small New England colleges, Rosie's passion and enthusiasm were contagious. Talking about art and the aesthetic experience was a gift from the Captain. His love of the masters and their depictions of the timeless, universal truths was one of the most enlightening-strikes of her life. From Rembrandt's *Night Watch*, Titian's *Bacchanal*, Durer's *Four Horsemen of the Apocalypse*, Ruben's *Garden of Love*, and Goya's *Third of May* she learned about humankind's tragedies, as well as its breathtaking beauty. For Rosie, the visual images were more powerful than the written word. In art history, the lessons she taught to her students were about understanding the continuum of traditions and styles. Not really lectures, more like down-to-earth conversations. First they stared long and hard at the artworks...and then she asked why...how does the subject and symbolism tell the story? She often left the students wide-eyed and shaking their heads. She reminded them time and again to "keep an open mind, this is not a judgment call on your part-just appreciate the art...and experience the color and shape relationships. It's fine if you hate it, that's your prerogative, but if you want to learn, allow your imagination to expand, make associations with the images and colors in your own life-it's the beauty of the design and universal truths that make the artwork worthwhile." Rosie even made up witty shortcuts and an Art History Time-Line Poster Calendar to help her students remember the dates, major art periods, and the artists' influences from one generation to the next.

For the cultures of the Fertile Crescent or Mesopotamia, she sang a bebop ditty with the abbreviation SABAP. And then for the six traditional American values, from the Colonial period to the twentieth century, it was FOWSCH or freedom, opportunity, wealth, self-reliance, competition, and hard work. It worked like a charm too, all the right answers showed up on the vocabulary quiz; SABAP was always Sumerians, Akkadians, Babylonians, Assyrians, and Persians. The acronym that really made them chuckle was DIC, for the three Greek orders—Doric, Ionic, and Corinthian. In America, the classical architectural elements are seen on all the important buildings- and in the Federal style, by the great Charles Bulfinch.

Rosie was only a B student in graduate school-and she swore to never be like her professors. She usually got put off during their lectures, for interrupting and asking too many questions. And her classmates didn't help either; "They all think they're smarter than me... but I'll get the same degree too," she vowed. Passing the master's examinations was like winging across the Grand Canyon and riding Niagara Falls all on the same day. It might have taken twice as long for her to comprehend the concepts and learn the dates, but that made her a better teacher. No high-falutin' elitist dialogues for Rosie; she made it simple-learn the vocabulary and figure out the story.

"And there's no such thing as a stupid question, stop me if you don't understand something...someone else probably wants to know too. Focus in on the details and keep asking why did they use those colors. There's really no right or wrong but the artwork does communicate the artists' ideas and societies' beliefs at the time. If you appreciate and understand art, the rewards are exhilarating-with a feeling of intelligence, understanding, and a new view of reality," Rosie proclaimed in every art history introduction class.

Art history is not just looking at beautiful pictures, as Rosie learned the hard way. It's a multi-disciplined field of archaeology, literature, philosophy, religion, and sociology. It's comparing styles, time periods, concepts, and traditions. Rosie was very visual; using her imagination was easy, it was the abstract concepts that were difficult. She always had to read the same thing over and over to remember it, even going so far as to create maps and diagrams of the major time periods to see the chronological order of art styles. The time-line poster was created for her students-since most everyone has trouble remembering historical events and dates. "Art is a product of its time, it tells a story......" she often repeated in class.

It was the iconography that was most fascinating-the legends, myths, and symbolism are the backbone of art history and the vertebrae are all the formalistic elements. The artists use shapes, lines, color, light, texture, and volume to bring about the image-to create the composition. Circles, spirals, and triangles are seen in all cultures, from the Buddha's wheel of existence to the Native Americans' circle dance. In the Classical style, the creative act intuitively unites balance, order, calm, and harmony; whereas passion, emotion, and color rule the Romantic style. Otherwise, it's often Realism-that nineteenth century movement in art and photography that sets the stage for everyone's favorite-Impressionism.

To look at the Captain and his search for the meaning of art is to believe in a do or die way of life. He was part bohemian, part temperamental artist, and part prisoner-caught up in the merry-go-round. His *Road Race* mural in the restaurant was a colorful celebration of family and life. Rosie was tending bar one afternoon, watching him paint it, when Alee came in asking for a Shirley Temple. "Oh, Great-Grandpap, you forgot me and Anna," she said. "No, no, dolly, you go next to your mom and dad on the roof, come and see it tomorrow," he chuckled, impressed at her close observation.

The Captain saw little six-year-old Alee as his Josie-all legs and eyes, full of energy and curiosity. But quick as a hummingbird's wings she was gone, soon to join Josie as two wiggling stars floating near Orion—tails intertwined.

A family run restaurant was a dream of Pat Merrick's-only it made his kids too dependent on him. There were no incentives for the boys, and they really thought that the restaurant was their inheritance. But after the thirty-year anniversary, it all began to unravel like a fishnet caught in a coral reef. First the Baron had to bail out his sons from gambling and unpaid bills-they fell under the spell of alcohol and the high life, rather than the bar business. The Baron abhorred taxes, and whiplashed his accountant into a fuzzy math scheme on how to avoid the labor and restaurant costs. It back-fired big time-when an audit revealed that he forgot to file for three years, and the fines had tripled by then—but of course he blamed the accountant.

The Baron was in a bit of a panic and decided he better sell before more crapola hit the fan, but instead he leased the restaurant to a small-time mafiosa type from South Boston. He avoided paying taxes for another year, and secretly negotiated to sell-while the kids worked in limbo, feeling humiliated, under the thumb of a new manager. Too bad the new "owners" stiffed the liquor and seafood companies, putting the Baron's reputation on the rocks. The sly fox even had Otis, a long-time adopted son, sign on as manager-owner one summer to dodge another IRS bullet. It took them years to figure out the money trail, and by then the Baron had died suddenly of a massive heart attack. Phelia had to get out or the IRS was going to chain the doors. She found a buyer pretty quick too, and almost finished the deal when she died just as suddenly, two weeks after the Baron, from lung cancer, and a broken heart.

Lily, Vera, and Rose wanted the Club to rise like a phoenix from the ashes after the funerals. But the brothers never got along and wouldn't let the girls run it, so the Cottage Club was finally sold. The sisters never trusted them to handle the money anyway-missing funds and cash from the safe was an everyday thing. It could have been declared a national historic landmark, being one hundred years old, but waiting for that to happen would have allowed the tax hounds to nip away at the Merrick kids forever. So the Cottage Club was sold for half its worth-to get out from under the Baron's mishaps and penalities.

The family fiasco with the will started to snowball when IOU notes were discovered in the Baron's safe. Resentment between the brothers was already as deep and silent as the grave. The oldest, Mark, owed the most-the ones that were signed and dated amounted to over twenty thousand. The sisters were always on each other's side with a bond stronger than Gorilla Glue. Rosie and Vera would have forgiven Lily's fifteen thousand in a heartbeat, but not Mark's. So they had to make it fair across the board, except when it came to Diane, the black sheep-there was nothing right about her unearned windfall. Like a termite who comes out of the woodwork, she showed up for the hearing.

Banished to Florida decades ago, schizoid Diane left her husband and two sons for a life of forged checks and heroin. Nevertheless, Pat and Phelia left her an equal share, despite her never working a day in her wasted life. The only job she ever had was being a pathological liar, and that requires skill in manipulation and planning for the next sucker. Ms. Delusional had conned everybody she ever met, from rehab counselors to psychiatrists. The pretty little blondie was performing like an actress at the age of twelve. But craving for more and more attention caused her to lose touch with reality-permanently. Pat and Phelia were just thankful she lived in Florida, where they often sent her cigarettes and money in jail. The greeting cards kept coming though, with more false promises than a politician. Selfish and without a conscience, Diane never blinked about her two motherless sons-but she got on her knees to become a re-born Christian ten times or more! She arrived after the funerals, not to say good-bye to Pat and Phelia, but to say hello to a bed of roses. Shaky and sober to boot, she sat quietly waiting for her sisters to challenge her share, but they never did. Foul as it was, Pat and Phelia had the last word and their children totally respected their wishes.

Brian was the executor of the estate, and guardian of Diane's slice. Not only was it a hard slap in the face to Mark, but to the girls as well-since Lily always had to fudge the register receipts, so Brian wouldn't get in trouble in the morning. The Baron even left a note in the safe one time, "Take the small coins and bills, Brian...leave the quarters and fives for me- Dad."

The next shocker came six months later when the new developer scheduled the legendary Club for demolition. Brian was in charge of the contents-photos, paintings, nautical objects, and antique Budweiser mirror-lights. He'd already made friends and deals with the new boss, hoping for a cushy job out of it, no doubt. Everything was gone in a week—everything except the name; the owner wanted that for posterity—it jacked up the price for his luxury seaside condos and drew customers to the Baron's once-great Cottage Club by-the-sea.

Dust to dust...and ashes to ashes, thought Rosie after the Davisville house went on the market, *and it all came tumbling down.* Lily and Vera couldn't even drive by the Club without tears blurring their vision, let alone drive by their parents' house.

Parked at the ball field one day, Rosie walked up to see the stone bench on the bluff named after her parents. She wandered down to the deck and peered through the dirt-caked windows-imagining people eating, drinking, and laughing, and then she saw the murals. "Those are not getting destroyed!" Rosie burst out loud. She called Lily up crying, "The place has been trashed...and they're not destroying Papap's murals!"

"No, no, Rose, don't worry...we'll get those off the wall. I'll call up Brian now and remind him again," Lily said firmly.

"Okay, coming over..." Rosie was calm by the time she got to the house.

Alee and Anna came running out in their bathing suits. "Aunt Rosie, let's go over to Nana's pool!"

"What? We can't...she's not there anymore. How about the beach instead?" Rosie asked. "Anyway, the pool's dirty."

The grandkids would never forget swimming in Nana's pool in the summer. Phelia would yell from the fence with a cigarette dangling in her mouth, "Hey Alee, do the back-float for me." In a second, she'd jump off the diving board, go down to the bottom to pick up coins, and be floating on her back like an angel-blue eyes staring at puffy white clouds. No doubt dreaming of her favorite place, a land of milk and honey-her Ambrosialand.

Rosie sat on the jetty the next day, waiting for Brian. She imagined the red tide spreading across the Sound, while Alee and the Baron stood together on the rocks. Then, looking up towards the deck she heard the reggae music playing for the Sunday Happy Hour. By saving the Captain's murals they would make sure that the Cottage Club would never be forgotten. The people in them tell about summers by the sea, full of family memories, as they enjoy a sun-filled, carefree life of plenty.

Beach Heights was like the Voyage of Life paintings by Thomas Cole, founder of the Hudson River School. This nineteenth century landscape series depicts four large Romantic scenes of man taking a symbolic journey on the River of Life. First an angel steers him through *Childhood* in a golden boat on a calm and clear day as he carries an hourglass full of sand. Then *Youth* takes over—while the angel waves from the river bank, he looks up at a castle in the sky and the waters begin to roll with whitecaps. During *Manhood* the angel is hidden in a dark and stormy landscape, while a man struggles to steer through a set of rapids. The hourglass is almost empty and the boat is breaking apart. In *Old Age*, a white-haired figure wrings his hands together in a final prayer, and the drifting boat quietly moves across a black, foggy river, while the golden angel in the sky points towards the heavens. Nature symbolizes our passages through life with her moods and waterways. Thomas Cole hopes we get the message with his landscape-metaphors for life's ups and downs. Art is forever warning us about the fleeting moments of time, as seen in many vanitas' still-lifes, genre paintings, and self-portraits. The cycles of nature—birth, growth, and decay—can be symbolized in the blasted tree trunks, crawling insects, butterflies, over-ripe fruit, and drooping faded flowers-traditional images and lessons to be learned. The Captain was right-artists are the best teachers and they speak a universal language.

Brian called from the deck, "Hurry up, Rose, before the trucks get here...they're coming for the barnboard." The race and harbor murals were all that was left of any value. Piles of broken glass, seashells, and beer cans made Rosie whisper, "Thank God the Baron didn't live to see this."

The murals were painted on sheetrock, then screwed into a wooden frame. They could not be peeled off; only a crowbar could jimmy them out of their frames. Rosie wasn't leaving without them-they were finally broken off in two pieces. But Brian decided to give them to the community center for the townspeople to enjoy. Immense pride and joy welled up inside of Rosie whenever she thought of them hanging up for everyone to see...especially the nights she taught art history upstairs.

Only the rec center kept them in the basement for years…until Vera and Teddy rescued them-proudly displaying them at home instead.

There was no time to get over the layers of misfortune heaped upon the Merrick siblings. Days before the arrival of the wrecking ball, the infamous Cottage Club got hit by the aftermath of Hurricane Dennis.

As fate would have it, the timing was uncanny-Mark had died suddenly, in the early morning hours, at the age of fifty-seven. He never lived to see the demise of his beloved stomping grounds, which may have been the thorn hidden in his side. They said it was a heart attack-brought on by late-night misadventures. He worked all his life for the Baron and helped make the Club one of the most successful rock-and-roll joints on the Cape. Mark was laughing on the outside and grinding his teeth at night. It was hard for him to look in the mirror and not see a failure, but he loved people and life too much, even more than taking care of himself-for his family. Everybody loved his sense of poetic justice and welcoming camaraderie, but the addictions trumped all else. He couldn't live with himself sober, and when you're in denial, getting high keeps the truth from knocking down the door. Mark even started on the Twelve Steps, and his dozens of journals found hidden in a closet prove that he kept trying and trying. But he never had a chance-the Cottage Club would only belong to Pat Merrick and never his sons. Mark's path of self-destruction was inevitable, along with his weak heart. Losing all of the Baron's good fortune was just too much to bear, and Mark escaped from this world, from the truth, way before his time.

The Baron rarely showed respect for his oldest son; mostly he held a fistful of IOU notes in his face instead. Maybe an intervention was the key for Mark, but all the life-threatening surgeries, combined with much substance abuse, kept getting in the way. Nothing could restore his broken dreams and body scars, especially the ones on his heart.

With a blurred mind and weak spirit, Mark never woke up that morning. Friends lined up around the block for hours to pay their respects.

At his wake the casket was closed, but everyone's hearts opened up-spilling out love and sadness over losing such a loving, generous soulmate.

The rise and fall of the Merrick clan was as impressive and tragic as that of the Crystal Palace. That's what the Cottage Club reminded Rosie of-a grand structure using new materials and entertainment for the masses. It was a revolution in architecture, like a giant greenhouse—satisfying the hungry and thirsty crowds who were searching for excitement, art, and a world's fair. The Cottage Club was a modern-day exhibition palace, not made of glass, like Joseph Paxton's 1848 original near London, but made of wood, and young fly-by-nights seeking adventure. During the war, the palace had to be dismantled, leaving its fragile beauty in pieces, as it happens in history-dozens of cultural landmarks become ravaged by fire and time, or, like the Cottage-Club, they just fall through the boardwalk cracks.

The Cottage Club played a major role in the community, and was a big hit in the "all the world's a stage" game. However, like Mark, Pat, and Phelia, nothing lasts forever, not even a hundred-year-old tradition. The Merrick family tree was getting smaller, and the only one who could handle all the sympathy and thank-you cards, phone calls and funerals, was Lily. She even took blurry-eyed Diane home for a while-until her pink cloud turned purple.

With her inheritance, Diane settled into an East Falmouth apartment. It was a godsend for her and Brian; money flowed out of her account like rain down a gutter-some for her every week, some for Brian. When the rehab clinics thought sociopath Diane was a medical miracle-for the one hundredth time-her money ran out fast. She had the HIV virus for God knows how long, and they also told her she had cirrhosis of the liver, and another drink would kill her. Still she sat night after night at the Amvets. After too many neighborly complaints and lost weekends, Brian moved her into a nursing home when she got pneumonia. Again she fell into a deep coma-they told us to come and say good-bye, but she rebounded as usual, again and again.

It wasn't long before Diane escaped from the nursing home, and later had to be committed to Bridgewater State Hospital for a thirty-day observation. She was in a lock-down now, a danger to herself with no place else to go. During the week, Lily got an early morning phone call from Diane's ex-husband Tim. "Hello Lily, it's Tim from Florida. Is Diane around?"

"Hi," Lily replied. "Well, yes and no, she's in the hospital right now. How are the boys?"

"Jamie had an accident—his car hit a tree late last night, and he died instantaneously...and never even got to the hospital."

Jamie Morris was the youngest son, and an amateur on the golf circuit by sixteen years old. He was more like his mother than anyone realized-resentful, alcoholic, and good-looking.

"What?Oh no, Tim, it can't be possible, he's too young..." Lily stopped short, thinking about everyone who had died. "What happened?"

"Can't really talk right now, Lily, but I warned him about drinking and driving. He wouldn't listen. He was always upset about something. He had a broken arm, too, and even his friends told him not to drive home. He lost control and went in a ditch," Tim explained. "Gotta go now, oh and it's okay, don't worry about coming down...just tell Diane for me."

The last time Rosie drove by the Cottage Club, there were piles of seaweed on the beach and a chain-link fence surrounding mounds of debris and rubble. *That's all that's left? After thirty years...then just nothing.* Rosie sighed and wiped her eyes hard. *It looks like one of Friedrich's existential, forlorn seascapes...a vast, empty space of ocean and sky where romantic longings run free, fleeing from a lonely world.* A rush of emotions and images washed over her: her father snapping his fingers to Frank Sinatra singing, "I Love York, New York," at 1 am for last call, her mother dancing the jitterbug to Beaver Brown. And throwing down shots of schnapps and kamikazes to entertain the bar crowd and feeling as famous as a queen for being a part of her father's dream-come-true castle-by-the-sea.

The first time Alee and Lily checked into Children's Hospital, weeks turned into months. They left only one time-three days before Halloween. And that was because every day, ten times a day, she begged the doctors in a scared, shaky voice, "When can I go home?"

Alee was a fighter, especially to the nurses, and she scowled at the doctors' orders-believing them less and less. She was punctured and x-rayed every day, right along with the daily blood transfusions, and a dripping bag of platelets-all to keep her little body working. Then there was Lily; not just her Mom, but her hot-pack and ice-chips specialist. Standing by her bedside, stubborn and determined to beat the cancer down, Lily never gave up hope, not until her Alee's last breath.

During every procedure, she'd be whispering in Alee's ear and holding her steady. "Go to that place, sweetheart, close your eyes and breathe deeply...imagine Nana's pool and you're swimming again." All the while, a team of doctors held her down and pushed a tiny plastic tube up into her nose, saying, "Swallow Alee, it has to go down your throat, to help your stomach...it's okay, it's almost over."

Gasping for air, in between her cries of, "Stop, stop, help me...I can't do it, no, no, don't, it hurts!" Lily stood firm and never panicked—but the doctors wouldn't stop until the tube hit her belly. She had to trust them, even though they never gave her any good news. It was more important to smile and be strong for Alee-to show her that it's going to be okay, that she'll win this fight. Alee would have died within a month, without the total body radiation-without her mother by her side. Meanwhile the most aggressive leukemia, AML, filled 85 percent of her body with poison cell blasts. It was just before her thirteenth birthday when they did the stem cell transplant from her brother Cody. When the cells took too long to grow, her bruised, swollen body went into limbo. But it wouldn't shut down because her young heart and clear lungs were too strong. Only the morphine drip slowed her down and eventually stopped her breathing.

When Alee walked out of the hospital for the last time, following her aggressive chemo and radiation treatments, she was thinking of what costume she would wear for Halloween. Not even her bald head and the intravenous line in her chest dampened her spirits. She was going home to see Dylan, her boyfriend, Cooper, her dog, and get her school photo taken-maybe even skate with her girlfriends. Trick-or-treat with her brother and sisters was just two nights away and the hospital was only a bad dream, so we all thought. Alee's Make-A-Wish had come true after all-to go home again.

The visiting nurses came daily that week, to give her meds and blood tests. At first Alee was smiling, free to be herself again. When she looked at her seventh grade school picture, her bald head made no difference. Her classmates had always looked up to her and still followed her around. Like the lonely boy who sent her a Valentine's Day card one year. Alee asked her teacher, "Why me?" "Because you are the most beautiful girl in class, kind and friendly.... and he loves you," she said.

Lily was raking leaves near the garden one day when Alee came over with Cooper. "Hey Mom, remember when we planted the pumpkins? And made the jack-o'-lanterns?" she asked.

"Oh yeah, honey, you loved to press the seeds in the dirt for me," Lily said, glancing down while her eyes filled up with tears. "Yeah, and when we picked them, the ladybugs flew off everywhere. I even caught two dragonflies that day for Vera," Alee chatted away. "She didn't like them in the jars, did she? Oh, gotta walk down to meet Dylan, be right back."

Lily watched her and Cooper walk around the corner out of sight and thought, *I'll never see her like this again. How did it happen that her time was over before it even began...* Lily sobbed until she saw them coming back-fixing the image in her mind forever, making sure it was etched clear as cut-crystal-remembering Alee's final days of freedom.

Even before the blood tests came back Alee cried easily and was sleeping most of the day. Lily figured she was getting worried and thinking too much about the hospital, and wondered what would happen if she had to go back again. Alee was super-sensitive and perceptive enough to know that there was one thing the docs weren't saying-like, don't worry... this will go away. She had no other choice, either scream and complain or take the medicine, "to get better." The blood tests came back and were disastrous—the worst news ever, for a cancer patient—Alee had a relapse. The blood cells were getting gobbled up by mutant runaway cytoblasts.

The very next day Children's Hospital notified Lily and requested that they return immediately. Lily told Alee that it was time to go back and get ready for the stem cell operation. Cody was coming too, for tests and blood work. Alee said nothing, but her face looked like an eagle had just plucked out her heart.

"Aunt Rosie's coming too," she yelled. "We're going to the museum to see Great-Papap's paintings. Tell them tomorrow, Mom, please."

"All right Alee, in the afternoon we have to be there for the doctors," Lily replied. "Better pack now for the morning...say good-bye to everybody tonight and I'll call Aunt Rosie."

Just the thought of a relapse sent Lily falling into a cold, dark well and she started hyperventilating. Rocking back and forth, she focused in on her breathing. "First the fungus and now a relapse," Lily moaned. Minutes later she was whispering to Rosie, "Gotta go back to the hospital in the morning...it's not a good sign, sis. Alee's been looking at the art text for days now, and wants to go to the museum with you first—to see the Captain's paintings."

"Okay, Lil, meet you there at nine on the nose...keep your hopes up."

The terror on Alee's face had faded and she looked as beautiful as a field of sunflowers. The van pulled in front of the museum where the Lakota Indian chief sat on his horse; Cyrus Dallin's *Appeal to the Great Spirit*, 1919. Alee jumped out first. Running over to Rosie, she stood on the steps. "What is the Indian doing?"

"Well, with his arms outstretched like that, what do you think?" Rosie asked.

"He's trying to talk to somebody...maybe, God, huh?"

"See how smart you are, Alee...yeah, his God is called the Great Spirit. Looks like he's asking for help," Rosie answered.

"I would like to ask for help, too, so I'm not sick anymore...can we pray to his Spirit or to Jesus?" She stared up to the sky and Rosie held her hand. Lily, Jack, and Cody came scooting over in time to hear Alee praying out loud... "God Spirit in Heaven, help my brother and me to be all right in the hospital and to get new cells again." Mother Nature stood still and a shaft of sunlight hit the Chief. Lily, Rosie, and Jack would have given up their lives, that minute, if only Alee could have gone on living a healthy life.

The colossal bronze doors opened up, they held hands and walked through the entrance. Slowly Alee turned and said, "Hey, it's time to go see...let's find Great-Grandpap's paintings."

Rosie announced to everyone, "It's always best to see the mummies first, since they are from the Ancient period...is that okay, Alee?"

"Yeah, but they look creepy 'cause they're dead and all."

"Listen for a minute, everybody eventually dies, but the Egyptians weren't scared, they lived on in the afterlife. The later mummiform coffins are really portraits of lesser kings and queens, ready for the afterlife and immortality. Their bodies are protected by special animals and insects painted on the sarcophagus. The symbols tell stories about their gods...and how their spirit lives on forever rising and setting with the sun."

"See those jars over there....the Canopic jars?" Rosie asked. "When the priests mummify the body they take out the lungs, liver, stomach, and intestines to preserve them. The brains are, well, not saved and the heart is perfumed and wrapped up in linen to go back inside the dried-out body."

"Aunt Rosie, they told us in school about pulling the brain out through the nose...it's so gross," Alee replied. "Glad they don't do that today. Does art always have to be about God and dying?"

"No, of course not, the Captain's paintings aren't about that...and oh, yeah, you know that the Olympics are starting soon, right? Well, the first games were in Greece about 776 BC—long after the Egyptians— and they didn't care about dying that much, only about sports and competition. You have got to see the black and red figure style Greek vases," Rosie exclaimed. "The paintings on the vases are full of stories about what the Greek people did for work and entertainment and how they did it. Also many scenes are about war and mythology. Don't look too close, 'cause some of the men are naked and running after each other," Rosie said.

"Oh that's okay, Alee," Lily said. "They're just playing a game."

"It's a bit more risqué than that," Rosie said.

"Never mind now," Lily replied.

Rosie led the way up the grand marble staircase, walking into a huge, double-hung European style gallery. Alee was beaming, like the time she went to her first dance with Dylan—getting her first kiss.

"Oh, look at the nudes, like in the book, Aunt Rosie—over here."

"Yep, that's Poussin's *Mars and Venus*—goddess of love with the god of war," Rosie explained. "Why do you think the artist put them together?"

Cody stood close enough to whisper, "Why are they naked?"

Alee quickly said, "That's the way they lived...they're not like us."

"This is a story from mythology—about the adventures of the gods and goddesses from Mt. Olympus," Rosie continued. "Venus takes the weapons away from Mars, as a symbol to make love and peace, not war.

"And Alee, remember the art poster I made? The names of the major periods...Classical, Medieval, Renaissance, Baroque, and Rococo?" Rosie asked.

"Yeah, it's hanging in my room," she replied. "But there's too many names and titles. The dates are confusing, too."

"Well, *Mars and Venus* comes from the Baroque period, when the styles and subjects were still traditional, based on the past, on history. This big word, *iconography*, is most important in art. It means to study the images, including the story and symbolism," Rosie explained. "So love and war, symbolized by male and female gods, are themes in life that affect people, and the painting's message is 'no more war.' "

Behind Rosie and Alee, Cody was asking Lily who that dead, naked man was with the nails at his feet. They turned around and Alee said out loud, "That looks like Jesus."

"It is, with the angels dressed in pink, yellow, and green," Rosie said. "The title is *The Dead Christ*...and he's monumental, bigger than life and taking up the whole painting. Fiorentino painted it during the Renaissance when religious art was number one...but this is more dramatic and strange for a Christ image, so they called it Mannerism, after the style of Michelangelo."

"Oh, he painted the ceiling, right, Aunt Rosie?" Alee asked.

"Excellent, honey, boy you really looked at those pictures...Leonardo, Michelangelo, and Raphael were some the greatest artists ever. And the Sistine Chapel ceiling is the story from the Bible, about the beginning of creation and the Fall of Man," Rosie preached. "Everything happened in the Renaissance, you'd love that time period...just look at Leonardo's rocks, clouds, and portraits....they come alive and makes us feel like we're there...understanding life and all."

Rosie put her arm around Alee and Cody, moving them through the gallery towards the Velasquez painting of Don Carlos and his dwarf. "Let's look at this one for a minute. There's two children, right? One is the future king of Spain and the other is, well, he's a dwarf...or a little person... can you see the difference?" Rosie inquired.

"And why would the artist even show them together like that?"

"Looks like they're playing together," Alee said. "But what are they holding?"

"Pretty good answer...Alee, the little boy in the back gave his little buddy a gold staff and ball to hold-symbols of royalty or his future status as a king." Rosie replied. "Velasquez was one of Spain's greatest artists—he was a court painter for all members of the family. His realistic style is exciting and full of hidden meanings. And the brushstrokes flicker across the surface, highlighting clothes, jewelry, and faces," Rosie rambled on.

Lily called from the end of the hall and motioned with her hand to come along.

"Okay, Alee, let's go to the nineteenth century...your Mom wants to get going," Rosie said. "And we have to find the Captain's works. Oh, but just look at this one...Turner's *Slave Ship*. The colors are brilliant, like a fiery sunset."

"What is that in the front?" Alee asked.

"It's pretty sad, honey. The story goes, there was a storm at sea and the captain threw the cargo overboard to collect the insurance money... but it was a slave ship from Africa-that's human beings with their legs in chains being attacked by sharks."

"Why would they do that?" Alee asked.

Rosie was sorry that she told the story, it wasn't the time to tell her about man's inhumanity to man...and the best part of knowing about history is learning not to make the same mistakes. "Don't know, honey," she said.

Walking through the museum made Alee forget she was sick for an hour. It was Rosie's shortest tour-but the one she'd always remember. Alee stopped quickly at *Flowerscape,* by Redon. "Look at all the fireflies and make-believe flowers...so dreamlike," she whispered.

"Hey Alee, let's go see the Impressionists and the Gauguin, before it gets too late," Rosie directed. "It's the big one over there. You okay? Feeling too tired?"

"Oh no, I'm okay..." Alee lied. "Oh, let's go and see the Captain's stuff...you know, the ones with all the people dancing...look that's modern art!"

"Really Alee, you like that abstract style?" Rosie exclaimed. "Wait a minute, you have to see the Gauguin first; about 'Where do we come from, what are we and where are we going?' His philosophy of life... look at the details...start from right to left. The young girl in the middle is searching or reaching for an answer, but who's in the beginning and the end?" Rosie asked. "You have to focus in on the details...what is that little thing in the right corner?"

"Well...it looks like a sleeping baby," Alee replied.

"Okay, and the girls are whispering about...probably love and life, even boys," Rosie said. "Now who's that crouching in the other corner... over here, Alee?"

"A grandmother...an old lady with white hair looking kinda sick."

"Yep, that's it...the story of how we come from a baby, grow up and wonder what are we here for, and then go back to nature and die. Artists have been painting this story forever," Rosie said softly. "Only some of us live longer than others...but we all go to the same place."

Staring at Gauguin's colorful but mysterious masterpiece was better than any school lesson—the facts of life pictured right before your eyes. The imagination is a far more powerful tool in teaching about ideas and themes. Art has always had that in-your-face presence—making the learning experience immediate and rewarding. Alee was getting the knowledge of a lifetime in a few hours. Rosie caught her twirling around in front of Degas's bronze ballerina...and the next minute she turned and stopped to look up at Renoir's *Bal a Bougival*. "What do you think the story is there, Alee?"

"Maybe he wants to kiss her or just dance, but she looks away..."

"And when you kiss someone usually that means..."

Alee shot back, "He loves her, right?"

"Oh, for sure, it's about love," Rosie replied. "And the yellow straw hat next to the red bonnet is just delicious."

Lily had been staying close by, watching Alee take it all in, and she whispered to Rosie, "Bet she would have been a dancer or some kind of performer...she always captivated everyone at the rink."

Rosie held back the tears and put her arm around Lily. "Well, honey, she's having the time of her life today," Rosie said.

"I'm getting worried about the doctors," Lily went on.

"You know, Lil, just let them wait...Alee will be their project again soon enough. We'll stay for another hour and get a bite in the cafe," Rosie announced. "Hey Alee, time to see some American art, that's where Great-Grandpap will be."

"Okay, but I want some french fries and chicken wings...let's go this way." And Alee was off skipping down the stairs with Cody at her heels.

"You guys follow me...see if you know who are in these portraits," Rosie instructed. "The artist is one of America's most famous...and everyone knows the story of the Midnight Ride of...Alee, think for a minute," Rosie asked, right away...but Cody yelled, "Hey that's Paul Revere!"

"Oh yeah," chimed in Alee.

"Why is he holding a teapot?" Rosie inquired.

"He's having tea....ha, ha," Cody laughed.

"No, not really, he made the teapot. Not only was he a patriot, but he was a silversmith, too. He's wearing the clothes of an artist, because he's proud of his craftsmanship," Rosie concluded. "John Singleton Copley painted most of the portraits in this room, and *Watson and the Shark* is his grand history painting for sure!"

"So the naked boy got eaten by a shark?" Alee asked.

"No, that's Watson when he was young...he lost his leg, but they saved him. Hey Alee, who's this a picture of...with the white hair?" Rosie pointed out and Alee, quick as a mouse, said, "That's George Washington, the first president."

"Wow, you're smart as the dickens, Miss Einstein," Rosie chuckled.

Lily smiled in awe at Alee and followed her into the next gallery-she was on a roll like Alice on her way through Wonderland.

They watched her walk slowly straight towards a huge landscape with a bright shaft of sunlight dividing the scene. "Aunt Rosie," Alee called, "see the two people standing with their arms raised up? And the yellow angel above?"

"Yeah, honey, that's a story from the Bible...about Adam and Eve going out of Paradise, painted by Thomas Cole." Rosie went on, "They disobeyed God and were punished...then had Cain and Abel, worked hard, and lived off the land."

"We always see a lot of paintings about God, huh?" Alee questioned. "Do you think it helps to pray?"

"Don't know for sure, Alee, but it can't hurt," Rosie replied.

"The priest comes to see me in the hospital, you know...he says God and his angels are watching over me...to make me better or to take me to heaven?"

"To make you better, of course," Lily joined in. "Now let's go look at the fisherman..."

"Oh yes, Winslow Homer loved the wildness of the ocean, and his realistic paintings of people playing outdoors tell the story of American life," said Rosie. "His *Fog Warning* shows the Baron's, and every fisherman's worst fear-caught at sea in the middle of a storm or lost in the fog."

Lily was looking worried and nodded her head for Rosie to move on. Alee started drifting and wandering over to the door. She stared long and hard at a huge painting dominating the back wall.

"Well, that's *The Daughters of Edward Darley Boit*, by John Singer Sargent," Rosie explained. "An American masterpiece and family portrait...What do you see, Alee?"

"All the sisters are hanging around, right?"

"Look closer, what are they doing?"

"Well, she plays with a doll, she hides her hands and looks shy...the two girls in back are talking," Alee answered. "Oh, yeah...they're different ages...it's about growing up, right?"

"Well, that's an excellent observation," Rosie replied, "and quite true, it's about the relationships of the sisters and what they do at different stages...it's so much more than a simple group portrait, and one of Sargent's most beautiful."

"Oh Alee, look at Niagara Falls, with the rainbow...which symbolizes hope and God's hand in Nature," Rosie exclaimed. "American artists worshipped the wilderness, especially the Grand Canyon and Niagara Falls-our very own natural wonders. Europe has temples, palaces, and classical ruins, but we have the greatest miracles of Mother Nature. Many nineteenth century landscape artists, from the Hudson River

School, claimed that God was present when the mountains, oceans, and forests were born."

Alee crinkled her nose and asked, "Think he'll come around and help me?"

"It's possible, but no one really knows for sure how he works things out... so maybe, honey," Rosie sighed. He did perform many miracles in his time...but you have to believe in him first."

Lily beckoned from the doorway and they all followed her out. The last gallery before the exit was twentieth century Modern Art. As soon as Alee feasted her eyes on the fanciful, brilliant colors in front of her, she called out, "There it is, hurry up, look at Great-Grandpap's picture! Aunt Rosie, that's it, right?"

"Well Alee, it looks expressionistic all right...but that's a Matisse... and right next to it is one by the greatest genius of the twentieth century—Picasso. What's that style called? Look close, try to see the subject..." Rosie instructed.

"The art book had a lot of strange pictures...it's the abstract style, right?" Alee replied.

"Be more exact, it begins with c..." Rosie coaxed.

"Oh yeah, that's Cubism, with small squares and triangles."

"Excellent, Alee," Rosie exclaimed. "Now, what is the story? The title says *Standing Nude*...do you see her?"

"Well, a little...the tan colors are like skin...is she dancing?" Alee inquired.

"Maybe, honey...wait, time to go, but look here first. Remember who the three fathers of Modern Art are? That's hard to think about...but sing it: 'Cezanne, Gauguin, and Van Gogh,' say it over and over so you won't forget-without them there could never be twentieth century abstraction and expressionism," Rosie announced. "Now let's go see Great-Grandpap's—there, it's called *Beach Heights Parade*."

"You might say this was one of his best ever...complete with all his favorite characters—strolling the boardwalk by the sea. The wonderful thing about the expressionistic style is how the artist's passion for his subject comes across through the bold colors in impasto, thick layered paint, mixed with decorative shapes." Rosie stopped to look at Alee, whose big, moon eyes were glued to the picture.

"They look happy...oh, see the names scribbled next to the people...and there's Great-Papap, 'Captain Bull Merrick 1972' in the corner!" Alee exclaimed.

"Yep, that's his signature all right...he finally got his name up there in lights, right next to the masters," Rosie announced.

Lily and the crew gathered round Alee to see her face shining like an opal-wet from her tears. Cody got close and hugged her, hoping his energy could shoot into her like lightning and kill the cancer. The moment became rolling snapshots of her life-but lasted only a minute. Lily stood speechless, fighting back tears and swallowing her cries. Rosie wanted to stop time and freeze Alee on the spot like a statue. *Instantaneity*...she thought, *capturing a fleeting moment in time like Monet's* Waterlilies...*air, light, and movement-Nature's most elusive qualities for life and Impressionism-except in Alee's case.* Lily called Alee from the doorway, breaking the stillness, and she turned, walking towards her, with the fluttering grace of Tinkerbell.

The only painting that stopped her short was Georgia O'Keeffe's *White Rose with Larkspur.*

"That's the biggest flower I've ever seen," Alee exclaimed. "It looks soft and fluffy like a cloud..."

"She was the greatest woman artist of the twentieth century," Rosie said. "And that's exactly what she wanted people to do...stop and look close-up, to see the heart of the flower."

Cody suddenly grabbed Alee's hand and yelled, "Aunt Rosie, Aunt Rosie, is that a bridge?"

"Yeah, at night...and very famous, called the Brooklyn Bridge. Look at the colors, Cody, it's America's greatest picture of progress, with fast-moving cars and red taillights reflecting off rows and rows of suspension cables. Joseph Stella's painting of New York is in the Cubist style-he was influenced by Picasso. The bridge is a Modern symbol of America's greatness–and a triumph of engineering," Rosie proclaimed.

"I'm getting tired, Mom," Alee whispered. "Think we better get going?" Rosie nodded to Lily and led the way towards the bronze doors.

"Are you ready, Cody?"

"Yeah, guess we'll be staying overnight," he replied.

"Oh yeah, they need your blood tests for the stem cells and all. Wait, what about the chicken wings? Maybe later," Rosie replied.

The mid-afternoon sun made its way across the grass, casting the Indian Chief in half-shadows. Lily held Alee's hand...and then gently knelt down to hug her. "Don't worry, sweetheart...you're going to be all right, Cody's going to give you brand new blood cells."

Rosie and Cody stopped and turned back to see them holding each other. "Everything okay?" Rosie called out.

"Oh yeah, Aunt Rosie," Alee said as she skipped lightly towards them. "That was one of the best times ever. Like my Make-A-Wish Disney trip, except this time we went around the world."

Even the best team of doctors couldn't save Alee. It wasn't that her fate was sealed, it was the poisonous cure—the cancer drugs that killed her. Lily carried her through though, cradled like a newborn, right up until the end. Alee looked at her mother and knew she was loved. It was her destiny to go and live in her Goldeanna Caves, that far-off, imaginary realm she had created for fun, with her friends. Only now it was forever—Alee's afterlife as Queen of Ambrosialand; "With a Smile in her Eyes, a Smile on her Lips, and Always a Kind Word too, So short a Life for One who Gave so Much to all She Knew."

THE BOSTON GLOBE

Names

CAROL BEGGY & STEPHANIE STOU

heavyweights at Jimmy Fund

Evander Holyfield with Amber Bailey at Dana-Farber's Jimmy Fund Clinic. Holyfield was in town for the "Making Better Communities" tour by Major Broadcasting Cable Network.

CHAMPS ON TOUR A day before bringing their message to Roxbury, five-time heavyweight champion **Evander Holyfield**, former New York Yankee **Cecil Fielder**, and chairman and CEO of Major Broadcasting Cable Network **Willie E. Gary** visited children being treated at the Jimmy Fund Clinic at the Dana-Farber Cancer Institute. Holyfield, Fielder, and Gary met with patients, signed autographs, and posed for photos. The group 4 Shades provided a special treat, singing a number of songs a cappella. The group is in the area as part of the cable network's "Making Better Communities" Tour 2002. Holyfield, Fielder,

Gary and **Marlon Jackson** (yes, as in the Jackson brothers) were in town to participate in an event Saturday at the Boys and Girls Club of Boston, Roxbury Clubhouse. The day is designed to empower people in urban communities with information to improve their lives. Friday's event also gave Jamaica Plain lawyer **Eddie Jenkins**, an independent candidate for Suffolk County district attorney, a chance to catch up with Holyfield. Jenkins, who played football for the Miami Dolphins (on the undefeated team of '72) and the Patriots, dates his relationship with Holyfield back to the champ's early fights for the title.

Palette of King Narmer-Hierakonpolis .... Egypt
Eannatum Stele-Telloh/Gudea Head .... Lagash
Zoser's Step Pyramid-Saqqara .... Egypt
Royal Standard/Gold Ram .... Sumer
Pyramids at Giza 'Old Kingdom' .... Egypt   2500 b.c.
Ankh Bust/Ti tomb relief (limestone) .... Egypt
Alaca Huyuk tomb-gold-Troy .... Anatolia
Akkadian Head-Sargon I/Naramsin Stele ...... Sumer

ANCIENT

Yellow River Valley Civilizations .... China   2000 b.c.
Indus Valley Civilization .... India
Sesostris Head-'Middle Kingdom' .... Egypt
Joman Period-clay figures .... Japan   1800 b.c.
Helladic Period-'Minyan Ware' .... Greece
Stonehenge .... England
Minoan Civilization-Knossos Palace .... Crete
Octopus Vase/Snake Goddess/Frescoes .... Crete
Hammurabi's Code/Portrait Head .... Babylon
Hittites 'Boghazkoy Gate' .... Anatolia   1500 b.c.
Amarna Period-'New Kingdom' .... Egypt
Funerary Temple of Hatshepsut-18th Dynasty .... Egypt
Ramses/Nefretti/Akhenaton/Tut's Tomb .... Egypt
Mycenaean Civilization-shaft graves .... Greece   IRON AGE
Vapheio Cups/Lion's Gate/Inlaid Daggers .... Greece   1200 b.c.
Assyrians-glass seals .... Mesopotamia
Shang Dynasty-bronze vessels/stone .... China
Celtic/Germanic Tribes .... Northern Europe
Hebrews-Israel/Phoenicians .... Lebanon   1000 b.c.
Asian Migration 'Bering Strait' .... North America
Geometric Period-Diplon Vase .... Greece
Chou Dynasty-bronze figures .... China
Chavin/Olmec-'Pre-Columbian' Culture .... America   800 b.c.
Ishtar's Gate/Neo-Babylonian .... Nineveh
Protocorinthian-'Chigi Vase' .... Greece
Protoattic Grave Vases-'orientalized' .... Athens
Thracian/Scythian Cultures .... S. Russia   600 b.c.
Etruscan Civilization .... Italy
Archaic Period-'kouroi' .... Greece
Black-figure vases/Coinage .... Athens
Temple at Aegina/Artemis Temple .... Corfu
Siphinian Treasury-'battle frieze' .... Delphi
Persepolis-Darius 'Hall-Achaemenid Art .... Persia
Basilica/Poseidon-'Doric'-Paestum .... Italy   500 b.c.

Zeus Temple-Olympia/'Kritios Boy' .... Athens   GREEK
Age of Pericles/Parthenon .... Acropolis   EMPIRE
Dionysus/Goddesses'frieze sculptures' .... Acropolis
Classic Period-'Doryphorus' .... Polyclitus
Propylaea/Erechtheum-Acropolis .... Athens
Discobolus by Myron/Dying Niobid .... Greece
Red-figure vases/pebble mosaics .... Greece   400 b.c.
Lysicrates Monument 'Corinthian' .... Athens
Mausoleum-Halicarnassus/Epidaurus Theatre .... Greece
Maurya Period 'Ashoka'-Buddhist Art .... India   300 b.c.
Chi'n Dynasty-'Wall of China' .... China
Hellenistic Period-'Alexander Age' .... Greece
Apollo/Venus/Nike-Praxiteles .... Greece
Altar of Zeus-Pergamon/Laocoon Group .... Greece
Han Dynasty .... China   200 b.c.
Ptolemic Period .... Egypt
Porta Augusta-Etruscan-Perugia .... Italy
Andhra Period 'Great Stupa'-Sanchi .... India

Pont du Gard/Mason Carree-Nimes .... France
Basilica/Forum-Leptis Magna .... North Africa
Imperial Period-'Colosseum' .... Rome
Titus' Arch/Pantheon/Trajan's Column .... Rome
Marcus Aurelius-equestrian statue .... Rome
Hadrian's Villa-frescoes/glass/mosaics .... Tivoli
Insula House-Diana-Ostia/Wedding Atrium ..... Pompeii
Judaic Art-'Duro Europus'-Sassanian Art .... Syria
Faiyum Portrait-'Egypto-Roman' .... Egypt
Shapur Palace in Ctesiphon .... Persia
Ajanta wall painting-'Hindu Art' .... India
Zapotec Civilization-'Classic Period' .... Mexico
Mayan Civilization-early period .... C. America

CHRISTIAN/BYZANTINE ERA

Arch of Constantine/Colossus Head .... Rome
St. Peter's Church/St. Paul's Basilica .... Rome
Catacomb paintings-SS Pietro .... Rome
Sta. Costanza-glass mosaics/murals .... Rome
Junius Bassus sarcophagus-reliefs .... Rome
Graeco-Roman-Bacchus diptych-ivory .... Rome
Gupta Dynasty-Buddha figures .... India
Vatican Vergil/Vienna Genesis-manuscripts .... Italy
Mausoleum-Galla Placidia-mosaics .... Ravenna
Byzantine Empire-'Justinian Age' .... Constantinople
S. Virale/St. Apollinare-dome mosaics .... Ravenna
Hagia Sophia-church/mosque .... Constantinople
Asuka Period-Korea/Nara Period .... Japan
T'ang Dynasty-Buddhist sculptures .... China
Madonna-'Graeco-Roman'-wood panel .... Rome
Celtic-Germanic Art-metalwork-Sutton Hoo .... England
Islamic Art-'Dome of the Rock' .... Jerusalem
Umayyad Dynasty-woven silks .... Persia
Great Mosque-Damascus/Mshatta Palace .... Jordan
Samarra Mosque-Iraq/Cordova Mosque .... Spain
Abbasid Period-'Baghdad Gate' .... Mesopotamia
Echternach Gospels/Anglo-Saxon Art .... England
Merovingian/Hiberno-Saxon Art-Book of Kells .... Ireland
Lindisfarne Gospels - 'Golden Age' .... Ireland
Carolingian Art-'Charlemagne'-Aachen .... Germany
Ebbo Gospels-Reims/Utrecht Psalter-manuscripts . Germany
Ottonian Art-Lindau Cover/Gero Cross .... Germany
Heian Period-wood sculpture .... Japan
Sung Dynasty-landscape/genre painting .... China
Paris Psalter/Harbaville Triptych .... Europe
Islamic textiles/glazed pottery .... Baghdad
Mozarabic Art-manuscripts/painting .... Spain

MEDIEVAL

ROMANESQUE

St. Michael's Cathedral-bronze doors .... Hildesheim
Abbey Church/Monastery-Cluny .... France
Pilgrimage churches-St. Martin/St. Sernin .... France
Hosios Lukas Monastery .... Greece
Westwork-Cologne/Florence Baptistry .... Italy
Bayeux Tapestry-embroidery .... England
Norman style-Jumiege Abbey/St. Etienne .... Caen
St. Mark's Cathedral-Venice/St. Ambrogio .... Milan
Romanesque wall painting-St. Savin Sur Gartempe .. France
Durham/Gloucester/Lincoln Cathedrals .... England
Cathedrals-St. Foy/Speyer/Tournai/Poitiers/Autun/Pisa
Romanesque sculpture-facade/St. Sernin/Souillac/Autun

B.C. A.D.

Sumer's 'Gilgamesh'	Trojan War	Greek Alphabet	Homer's	Democratic 508 b.c.	Punic Wars
1st Writing-3000 b.c.	1185 b.c.	800 b.c.	Illiad 750 b.c.	Gov't-Athens	264 b.c.
Persians settle	Latins settle Rome	Buddha born	Indian 355 b.c.	Socrates/Plato	
Iran 2000 b.c.	1300 b.c.	Confucius born China		Aristotle-350 b.c.	
Abraham leads		1st Olympics	Roman Republic	Alexander the Great	
Hebrews to Canaan 1900 b.c.		776 b.c.	500 b.c.	336 b.c.	

Julius - 61 a.d.	Edict of Milan	Muhammad born Mecca	Charlem
Caesar rules	313 a.d.	founds Islam - 570 a.d.	Roman I
Jesus Christ	Ptolemy	Goths sack	Moors invade
crucified-30 a.d.	180 a.d.	Rome - 410 a.d.	Spain - 710
Pompeii	St. Patrick in		Iconoclasm	V
erupts - 79 a.d.	Ireland - 400 a.d.		720	inv

* FIRST PART of "ART HISTORY" TIME-LINE POSTER by S. SWEENEY REILLY 1986

Art References

S. SWEENEY

PART I

Art History Time-Line Calendar poster, 1986
Pieter Brueghel, *The Fall of Icarus*, 1560
Van Gogh, *Starry Night*, 1889
El Greco, *The View of Toledo*, 1610
Frans Hals, *The Regentesses*, 1664
Titian, *Rape of Europa*, 1569
Hokusai, *The Great Wave*, 1831
Van Gogh, *Crows Over the Wheat Field*, 1890
Michelangelo, *The Pieta*, 1504

PART II

Albrecht Durer, engraving of Adam and Eve, 1501
Theodore Gericault, *The Raft of the Medusa*, 1818
William Hogarth, *The Rake's Progress*, 1734
Degas, *The Absinthe Drinker*, 1876
Toulouse-Lautrec, *At The Moulin Rouge*, 1889
Book of Kells, c.800 AD
Willem de Kooning, *Woman I*, 1952
Joan Miro, *The Carnival*, 1921
Paul Gauguin, *Tahitian Woman/Day of the God*, 1893
Botticelli, *Birth of Venus Primavera*, c.1482
Bosch, *Garden of Earthly Delights*, c.1500
Rembrandt, *Return of the Prodigal Son*, 1669

Hannah Hoch, *Cut with the Kitchen Knife,* 1919

Hokusai, *The Wave 1831*

PART III

Goya, *The Sleep of Reason Produces Monsters,* 1799

Goya, *Saturn Devouring His Son,* 1820

Van Gogh, *Irises,* 1888

Michelangelo, *Bound Slaves,* 1510

Bosch, *The Garden of Earthly Delights,* c.1500

Gauguin, *Day of The God,* 1896

Degas, *The Absinthe Drinkers,* 1876

ART REFERENCES-PART IV

Mark Rothko, *Blue and Green,* 1955

Max Ernst, *Elephant of Celebes,* 1919

Rene Magritte, *Eyeball in the Sky,* 1928

Dali, *The Persistence of Memory,* 1936

Joseph Mallord William Turner, *The Slave Ship,* 1840

Leonardo da Vinci, *The Mona Lisa,* 1504

Frans Hals, *Jolly Toppers,* 1660

Vincent van Gogh *Starry Night* 1890

PART V

Ruben, *Garden of Love,* 1638

Velasquez, *Las Meninas,* 1656

Caravaggio, *Bacchus,* 1595

Manet, *Bar at the Folies Bergere,* 1882

Vermeer, *Concert,* 1664

Rembrandt, *The Mill,* 1660

Picasso, *Guernica,* 1937

William Blake, *Whirlwind of Lovers,* 1795

Michelangelo, *David,* 1500-4

Matisse, *The Dance,* 1906

Rousseau, *The Dream,* 1910

Picasso, *Girl Before a Mirror,* 1936

Chagall, *Lovers with Birds,* 1910

Gauguin, *Tahitian Girl,* 1897

Munch, *The Scream,* 1893

Nicholas Poussin *Mars and Venus* (MFA-Boston) c.1630

Rosso Fiorentino, *The Dead Christ,* 1524

Michelangelo, Sistine Chapel ceiling, 1508-12

Diego Velasquez, *Don Carlos Balthaser,* 1656

Turner, *The Slave Ship,* 1840

Odilon Redon, *Flowerscape* (MFA-Boston), 1903

Paul Gauguin, *Where do we come from? What are we? Where are we Going?* (MFA-Boston), 1897

Degas, *Ballerina,* 1875

August Renoir, *Bal a Bougival,* 1883

John Singleton Copley, *Paul Revere / Watson and the Shark,* 1778

Thomas Cole *Adam and Eve,* 1828

Winslow Homer, *Fog Warning* (MFA-Boston), 1885

John Singer Sargent, *The Daughters of Edward Darley Boit,* (MFA-Boston), 1882

Picasso, *Standing Nude* (MFA-Boston), 1908

Captain Joe Miron, *Beach Heights Parade,* 1949

Claude Monet, *Waterlilies,* (MFA-Boston), 1920

Georgia O'Keeffe, *White Rose & Larkspur,* (MFA-Boston), 1927

Joseph Stella, *The Brooklyn Bridge,* (MFA-Boston), 1917

Rembrandt, *Night Watch,* 1640

Titian, *Bacchanal,* 1510

Albrecht Durer, *Four Horsemen of the Apocalypse,* 1497

Ruben, *Garden of Love,* 1639

Francisco Goya, *The Third of May,* 1808-1814

Thomas Cole, *Voyage Of Life* (4 landscapes), 1826

Cyrus Dallin's, *Appeal to the Great Spirit*, 1919

PERSONAL REFERENCES
BACK COVER

1. Alee at Children's Hospital with Rosie, Lily, Vera and Jack (pencil drawing by S. Reilly 2005)

2. Jerry, Cody, and Kathy Bailey 2000

3. Amber with Nurse 2002

4. Family Photo at the Sweeneys' 1978 (The Merricks)

5. *Starry Night* by Vincent van Gogh 1890

6. Vera and Bill Sweeney at Ya-Ta-Hay Indian Shop 1978 (Phelia and Pat Merrick)

7. *Nobska Point* –watercolor by Captain Joe Miron 1972

8. *Self-portrait* by S. Reilly 1974

9. Casino mural of *Boats and Harbors* by Captain Joe Miron 1976

10. Wharf solarium with Captain self-portrait 1965

11. Sisters photo – Sandra, Suzanne, and Kathy 2001 (Vera, Rosie, and Lily)

12. Casino Wharf Restaurant-Grand Avenue, Falmouth Heights 1999

13. Paul J. Reilly photo 2001 (Sean Malone)

14. Native American Seasonal Full Moons poster by S. Reilly 2000

15. The Baron's Casino "fishing machine" unloading sharks 1990

16. Spanky and Beansie Reilly photo in 2001

17. *Fishing on the Island* by Captain Joe Miron 1952

18. *At the Moulin Rouge* by Toulouse Lautrec 1892

19. Casino mural of *New Bedford Harbor & Sailing* by Captain Miron 1979

20. Leonardo da Vinci's *Mona Lisa* 1503

21. The Captain's treasure map found by Alee in the studio

22. Amber's photo of her favorite blue butterfly 2000
23. Photo of Casino Wharf Finish-Line on Road Race –1985 (The Cottage Club in Beach Heights)
24. Photo of three sisters and three sisters 1999-

Amber, Hannah, and Emma / Kathy, Sandy, and Suzy

25. *The Harlequin's Carnival* by Joan Miro 1932
26. *The Raft of the Medusa* by Theodore Gericault 1824
27. *The Birth of Spring* or *Primavera* by Botticelli 1482
28. *The Garden of Earthly Delights* by Hieronymus Bosch c.1500 with Paradise/Earth/Hell panels
29. Raphael's fresco—School of Athens 1510
30. Paul Gauguin's *Where do We Come From, What Are We, Where are We Going* 1897

WHY DO I RELAY? by Hannah Bailey

RELAY FOR LIFE Race

You ask us the question that really has no answer

Do you do it for friends, family, or to just find a cure for cancer

Well, to me I relay for the feeling of getting something out

For helping someone is what it's really about

This relay means so much to me, people show how much they care

All you have to do is put a hand out for someone to spare

I relay for knowing I'm helping someone in any way

"You're really doing a lot" is what they would say

The word "HOPE" on the shirts really does describe it all

You have to get out there and really have a ball

This isn't asking much, just a little of your time

Even a little of donations is not a crime

Some people relay for someone they care for, admire, or love

Some people have made it and some have gone above

My sister passed away of leukemia in 2003

And this is why this relay means so much to me!